CONTENTS

Initial, Medial, Final Consonants

UNIT 1 — Theme: All Around Town

Poem "The Folk Who Live in Backward Town" by Mary Ann Hoberman 3
Home Letter 4
Initial and Final Consonants 5-10
Medial Consonants 11-12

Review Initial, Medial, Final Consonants
Phonics & Spelling: Consonants 13
Phonics & Writing: A Description 14
Take-Home Book: *Meet My Town* 15-16
Unit Checkup 17-18

Short Vowels

UNIT 2 — Theme: Fun in the Sun

Activity Hidden Pictures 19
Home Letter 20
Short Vowel **a** 21-24
Short Vowel **i** 25-28
Review Short Vowels **a, i** 29-30
Short Vowel **u** 31-34
Review Short Vowels **a, i, u**
Phonics & Reading: "Ball Games" 35

Phonics & Writing: A Description 36
Short Vowel **o** 37-40
Short Vowel **e** 41-44
Review Short Vowels **a, i, u, o, e**
Phonics & Spelling: Short Vowels 45
Phonics & Writing: A Postcard 46
Take-Home Book: *Twists on Tag* 47-48
Unit Checkup 49-50

Long Vowels

UNIT 3 — Theme: On Wings and Wheels

Poem "I Like to Go Places" 51
Home Letter 52
Long Vowel **a** 53-54
Long Vowel **i** 55-56
Review Long Vowels **a, i** 57-58
Long Vowel **u** 59-60
Review Long and Short Vowels 61-62
Review Long Vowels **a, i, u**
Phonics & Reading: "Playing for the President" 63

Phonics & Writing: A Narrative 64
Long Vowel **o** 65-66
Review Long Vowels **a, i, u, o** 67-68
Long Vowel **e** 69-70
Review Long and Short Vowels 71-72
Review Long Vowels **a, i, u, o, e**
Phonics & Spelling: Long Vowels 73
Phonics & Writing: A Description 74
Take-Home Book: *So Many Sights to See* ...75-76
Unit Checkup 77-78

Compounds; Le Words; Hard and Soft c, g; Blends; Y as a Vowel; Digraphs; R-Controlled Vowels

UNIT 4 — Theme: The World Outside

Activity What's Wrong with This Picture? 79
Home Letter 80
Compound Words 81-82
Two-Syllable Words 83-84
Words Ending in **le** 85-86
Hard and Soft **c, g** 87-90
Review Hard and Soft **c, g** 91-92
Review Compounds; Syllables; **le**; Sounds of **c, g**
Phonics & Reading: "Jack and the Beanstalk" 93
Phonics & Writing: A Story 94
R Blends 95-96

L Blends 97-98
Review **r** and **l** Blends 99-100
S Blends 101-102
Final Blends 103-104
Review Blends
Phonics & Reading: "Sunflowers" 105
Phonics & Writing: A Description 106
Y as a Vowel 107-110
Review Compounds; Syllables; **le**; Hard and Soft **c, g**; Blends, **y** as a Vowel
Phonics & Spelling: Compounds; **le**; Hard and Soft **c, g** Syllables; Blends; **y** as a Vowel 111

Phonics & Writing: A Story 112
Take-Home Book: *Johnny Appleseed* . . . 113-114
Consonant Digraphs **sh, th, wh, ch** 115-116
Consonant Digraphs **sh, th, wh, ch, ck** . . 117-118
Consonant Digraph **kn** 119-120
Consonant Digraph **wr** 121-122
Review Digraphs
Phonics & Reading: "Chipmunks" 123
Phonics & Writing: A Description 124

R-Controlled Vowels **ar, or** 125-128
R-Controlled Vowels **ir, er, ur** 129-130
Review **r**-Controlled Vowels 131-132
Review Digraphs and **r**-Controlled Vowels
Phonics & Spelling: Digraphs, **r**-Controlled
Vowels 133
Phonics & Writing: A Newspaper Story . . . 134
Take-Home Book: *The Talking Forest* . . . 135-136

Unit Checkup 137-138

Contractions, Endings, Suffixes

UNIT 5 — Theme: Blasting Off

Poem "Countdown" 139

Home Letter 140

Contractions with **will, not, is, have** . . . 141-144
Contractions with **am, are, us, is, will** . . 145-146
Review Contractions
Phonics & Reading: Letter from Space Camp 147
Phonics & Writing: An Application 148
Plural Endings **s, es** 149-150
Inflectional Endings **ing, ed** 151-152
Review Endings **s, es, ing, ed** 153-154
Inflectional Endings **ing, ed**; Doubling Final
Consonant 155-156
Inflectional Endings **ing, ed**; Drop Final **e** . . .157-158

Review Endings **s, es, ing, ed**
Phonics & Reading: "Seeing Stars" 159
Phonics & Writing: A Journal 160
Suffixes **ful, less, ness, ly** 161-163
Review Suffixes **ful, less, ness, ly** 164-166
Suffixes **er, est** 167-168
Suffixes **er, est** with Words Ending in **y** . 169-170
Suffixes **es** with Words Ending in **y** 171-172
Review Endings, Suffixes
Phonics & Spelling: Endings, Suffixes 173
Phonics & Writing: A Sign 174
Take-Home Book: *In Space* 175-176

Unit Checkup 177-178

Vowel Pairs, Vowel Digraphs, Diphthongs

UNIT 6 — Theme: Dinosaur Days

Poem "Dinosaur Museum" 179

Home Letter 180

Vowel Pairs **ai, ay** 181-182
Vowel Pairs **ee, ea** 183-184
Vowel Pairs **ie, oe, oa, ow** 185-186
Review Vowel Pairs **ai, ay, ee, ea, ie, oe, oa, ow**
Phonics & Reading: "Kay's Surprise" 187
Phonics & Writing: A Thank-You Note 188
Take-Home Book: *The Apatosaurus* 189-190
Vowel Digraph **oo** 191-192
Vowel Digraph **ea** 193-194
Vowel Digraphs **au, aw** 195-196
Review Vowel Digraphs **oo, ea, au, aw** . . 197-198

Review Vowel Pairs and Digraphs
Phonics & Reading:
"What Really Happened?" 199
Phonics & Writing: A Newspaper Story . . . 200
Take-Home Book: *Dean's Day Out* 201-202
Diphthongs **ou, ow** 203-206
Diphthongs **oi, oy** 207-210
Diphthong **ew** 211-212
Review Vowel Pairs, Digraphs, Diphthongs
Phonics & Spelling: Vowel Pairs, Digraphs,
Diphthongs 213
Phonics & Writing: A Rhyme 214
Take-Home Book: *Dinosaur Riddles* . . . 215-216

Unit Checkup 217-218

Prefixes, Synonyms, Antonyms, Homonyms

UNIT 7 — Theme: Make It, Bake It

Poem "Origami" 219

Home Letter 220

Prefixes **re, un, dis** 221-226
Review Prefixes **re, un, dis** 227-228
Synonyms 229-230
Antonyms 231-232
Homonyms 233-234

Review Prefixes, Synonyms, Antonyms, Homonyms
Phonics & Spelling: Prefixes, Synonyms,
Antonyms, Homonyms 235
Phonics & Writing: A Description 236
Take-Home Book:
Make Your Own Play Dough 237-238

Unit Checkup 239-240

Definitions and Rules

Read Aloud

The Folk Who Live in Backward Town

The folk who live in Backward Town
Are inside out and upside down.
They wear their hats inside their heads
And go to sleep beneath their beds.
They only eat the apple peeling
And take their walks across the ceiling.

Mary Ann Hoberman

▶ Talk about some of the funny things in the poem.

THINK! Why is the town named Backward Town?

Home Letter

Dear Family,

During the next few weeks, we're going to be learning about letters and sounds at the beginning, middle, and end of words. We'll also be talking about our neighborhood and community.

At-Home Activities

Here are some activities you and your child may enjoy doing together.

▶ Make a list of places to visit in your town. Ask your child to draw a picture of his or her favorite place in town.

▶ Take a walk through town with your child. As you go, point out words on signs, buildings, and stores. Read the words and have your child identify the letters for the beginning and ending sounds.

Book Corner

You and your child might enjoy reading these books together.

Cool Ali
by Nancy Poydar
Ali's drawings help her neighbors beat the heat on a summer day in the city.

How to Get Famous in Brooklyn
by Amy Hest
Janie records all of the things that happen in her neighborhood until the wind blows away her papers.

Sincerely,

Say the name of each picture. Print the capital and small letters for its beginning sound.

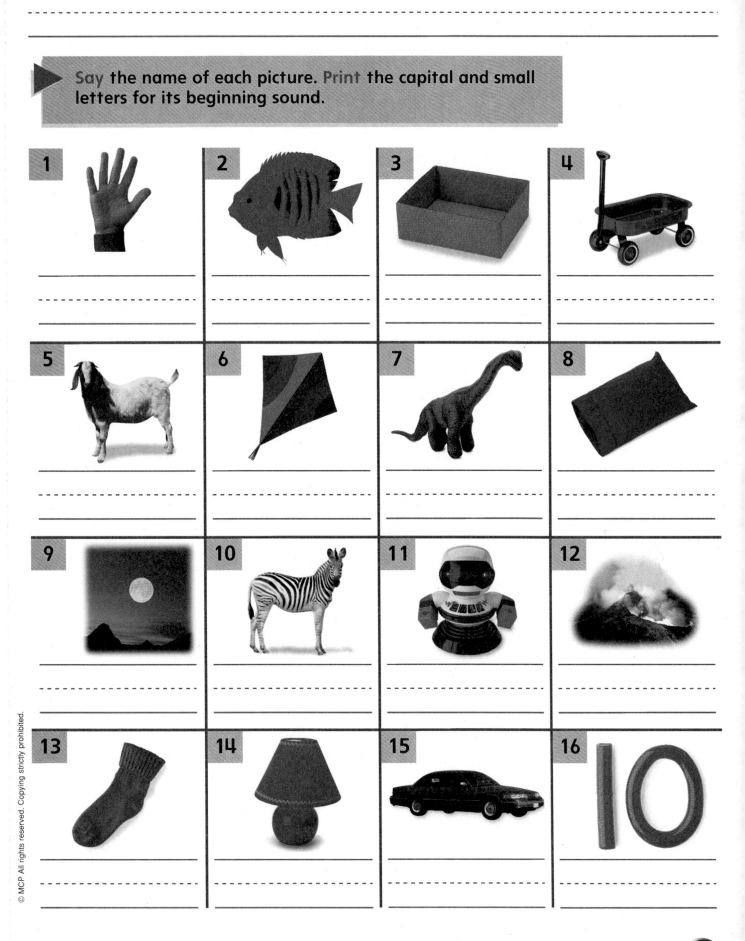

1

2

3

4

5

6

7

8

9

10

11

12

13

14

15

16

Initial consonants: Phonemic awareness

Say the name of each picture. Print the letter for its beginning sound. Trace the whole word.

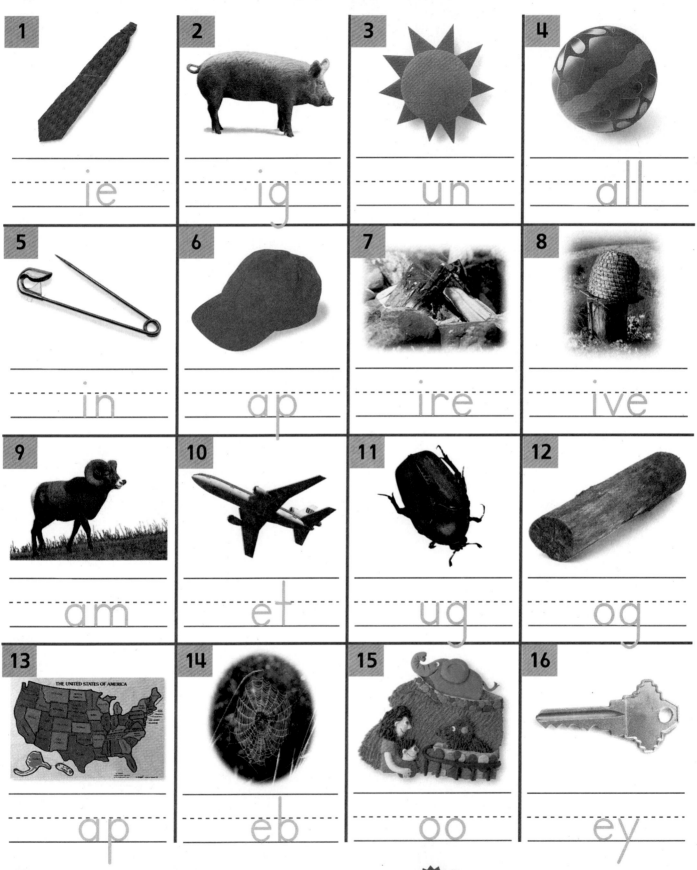

1 ie

2 ig

3 un

4 all

5 in

6 ap

7 ire

8 ive

9 am

10 et

11 ug

12 og

13 ap

14 eb

15 oo

16 ey

Home

Ask your child to name another word with the same beginning sound as each word pictured.

Say the name of each picture. Print the letter for its ending sound.

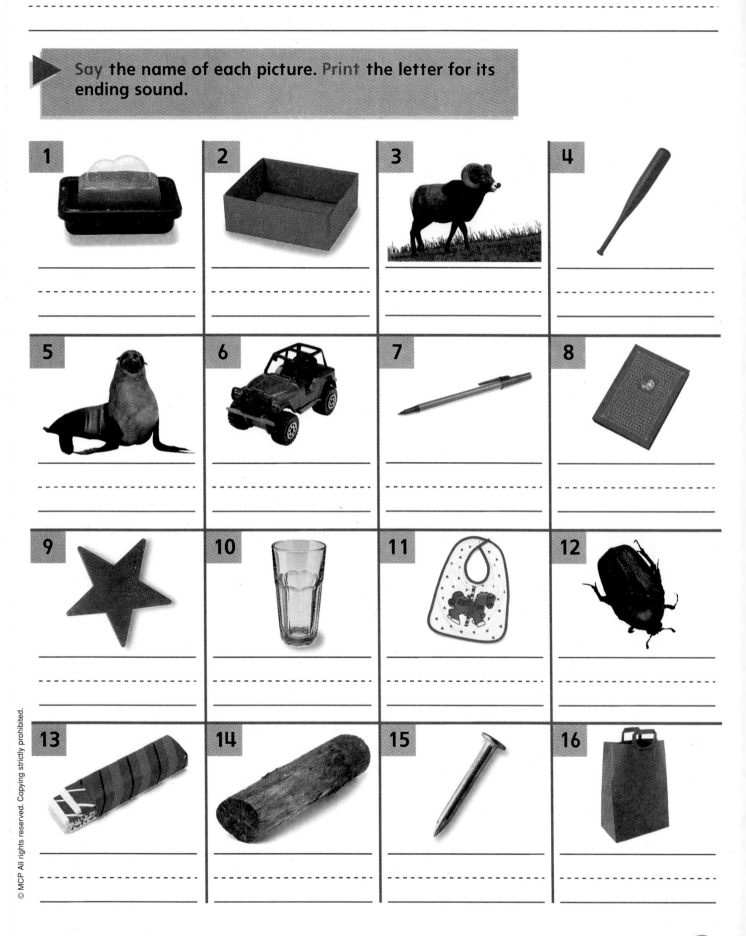

1

2

3

4

5

6

7

8

9

10

11

12

13

14

15

16

Lesson 2
Final consonants: Phonemic awareness

7

Say the name of each picture. **Print** the letter for its ending sound. **Trace** the whole word.

1 ma	**2** we	**3** do	**4** be
5 sai	**6** cu	**7** su	**8** bu
9 ha	**10** lea	**11** bo	**12** dru
13 li	**14** bow	**15** bir	**16** ja

Lesson 2
Final consonants: Spelling

Home

Ask your child to name the pictures whose names have the same ending sounds.

Change **the letters to make new words.**
Write the words on the lines.

cat

1. Change the **c** in **cat** to **m**.

2. Change the **t** to **p**.

3. Change the **m** to **l**.

4. Change the **p** to **d**.

5. Change the **l** to **m**.

6. Change the **d** to **n**.

7. Change the **m** to **r**.

8. Change the **n** to **t**.

Say the name of each picture. Print the letter for its beginning sound. Then print the letter for its ending sound. Trace the whole word.

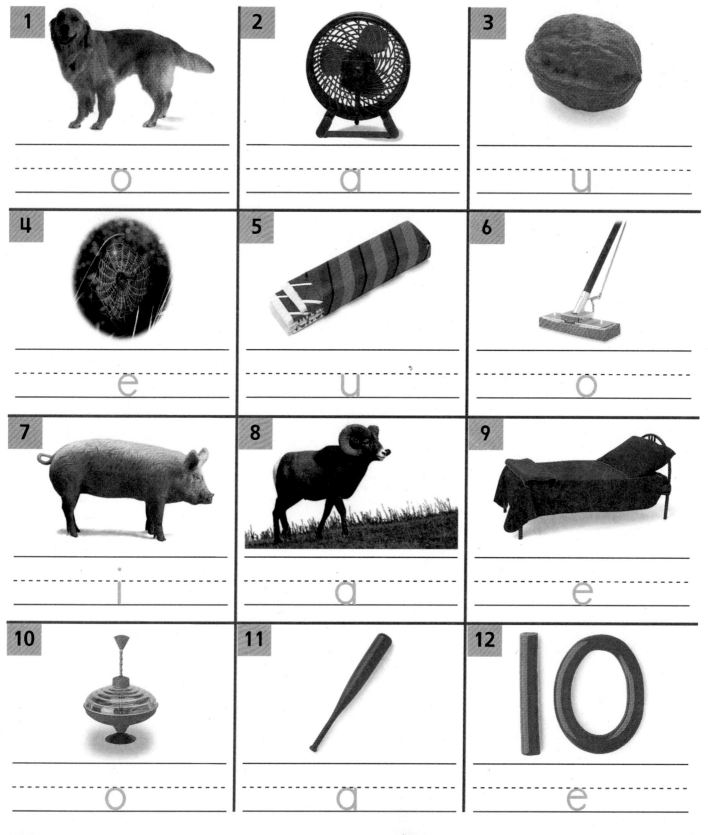

1   o

2   a

3   u

4   e

5   u

6   o

7   i

8   a

9   e

10   o

11   a

12   e

Lesson 3
Initial and final consonants: Spelling

Say a word and have your child think of another word that has the same beginning or ending sound.

Say the name of each picture. Print the letter for its middle sound.

1

2

3

4

5

6

7

8

9

10

11

12

13

14

15

16

Lesson 4
Medial consonants: Phonemic awareness

Say the name of each picture. **Print** the letter for its middle sound. **Trace** the whole word.

1 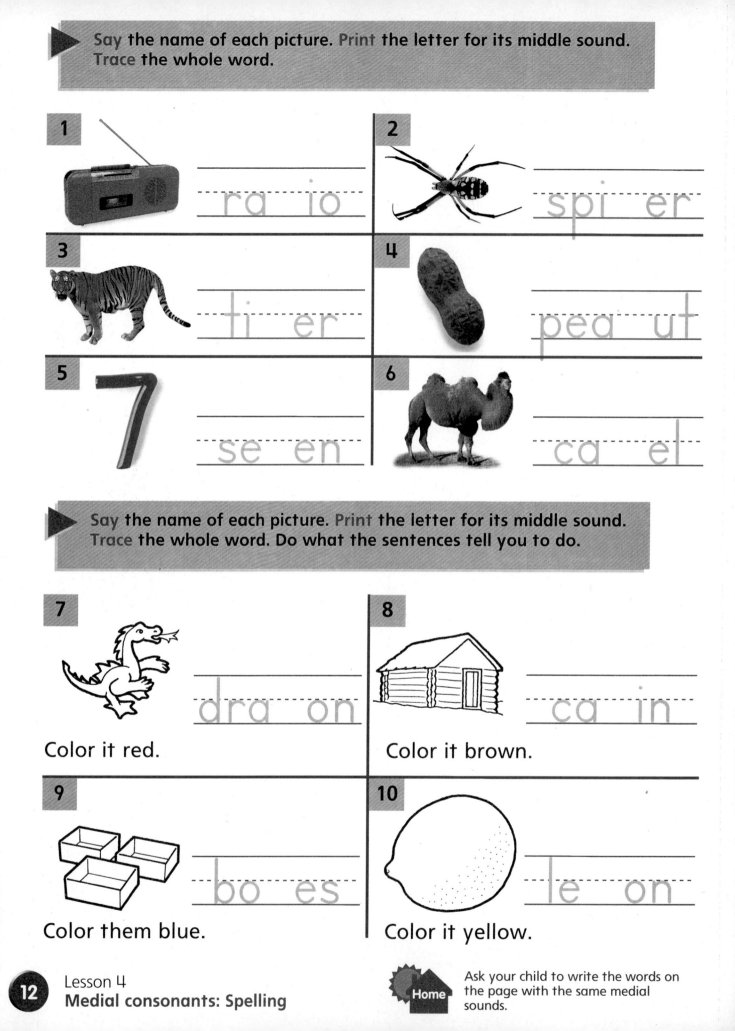 ra ⸀ io

2 spi ⸀ er

3 ti ⸀ er

4 pea ⸀ ut

5 se ⸀ en

6 ca ⸀ el

Say the name of each picture. **Print** the letter for its middle sound. **Trace** the whole word. Do what the sentences tell you to do.

7 dra ⸀ on

Color it red.

8 ca ⸀ in

Color it brown.

9 bo ⸀ es

Color them blue.

10 le ⸀ on

Color it yellow.

12
Lesson 4
Medial consonants: Spelling

Home
Ask your child to write the words on the page with the same medial sounds.

Phonics & Spelling

Read each sentence. To finish the sentence, use the mixed-up letters in the box to make a word. Print the word on the line.

THE MARKET

1. Jed wants to get bubble _____. | ugm |

2. Pam wants to buy that cute pink _____. | gpi |

3. I wonder what's in that big _____? | oxb |

4. Mom wants a yellow _____. | elmno |

5. Did Dad find a _____ of jam yet? | raj |

6. I will buy this blue _____. | pne |

7. Look, there's a spider _____! | bwe |

8. Is there a _____ in it? | edrips |

9. I _____ that's not for sale! | ebt |

THINK! Where are they?

Phonics & Writing

Write about a place in your neighborhood that you like. Tell where it is and what you do there. Then tell why you like it. Use some of the words in the box.

gum	store	spider	ride	park
yard	bus	house	library	box
school	porch	web	play	robot

_____

- -

_____

- -

_____

- -

_____

- -

_____

- -

_____

Book Corner

Mrs. Tuck's Little Tune
by Cass Hollander

Mrs. Tuck's tune is passed from one person to another until the whole community is humming it.

Lesson 5
Initial, medial, final consonants: Writing

Home

Ask your child to name the letters at the beginning, middle, and end of some of the words he or she wrote.

TALK ABOUT IT

Who is in your family?
What do you like to do
together?

8

This book belongs to:

_____

- - - - - - - - - - - - - - - - - -

_____

1

Meet all my family. This is my
sister, Meg. That is our dog,
Tiger. Have I left anyone out?

6

This is my school. You can find
me here five days a week. I
painted the red dragon.

3

Meet my dad. He drives a taxicab all around the town. I like to go with him.

2

Oh, yes! Meet me—Jim! How do you like my pictures?

7

My town is not very big, but it has a lot of shops. You can get fish or milk. You can get a drum or a dress.

4

Meet my mom. She plays music and talks on the radio.

5

> **Say the name of each picture. Fill in the bubble beside the letter for the beginning sound of the word.**

1.
- ○ b
- ○ g
- ○ d

2.
- ○ k
- ○ m
- ○ y

3.
- ○ w
- ○ r
- ○ t

4.
- ○ w
- ○ l
- ○ m

> **Say the name of each picture. Fill in the bubble beside the letter for the ending sound.**

5.
- ○ b
- ○ l
- ○ s

6.
- ○ d
- ○ x
- ○ g

7.
- ○ m
- ○ b
- ○ x

8.
- ○ m
- ○ p
- ○ b

> **Say the name of each picture. Fill in the bubble beside the letter for the middle sound.**

9.
- ○ r
- ○ c
- ○ b

10.
- ○ c
- ○ t
- ○ r

11.
- ○ m
- ○ n
- ○ l

12.
- ○ r
- ○ d
- ○ l

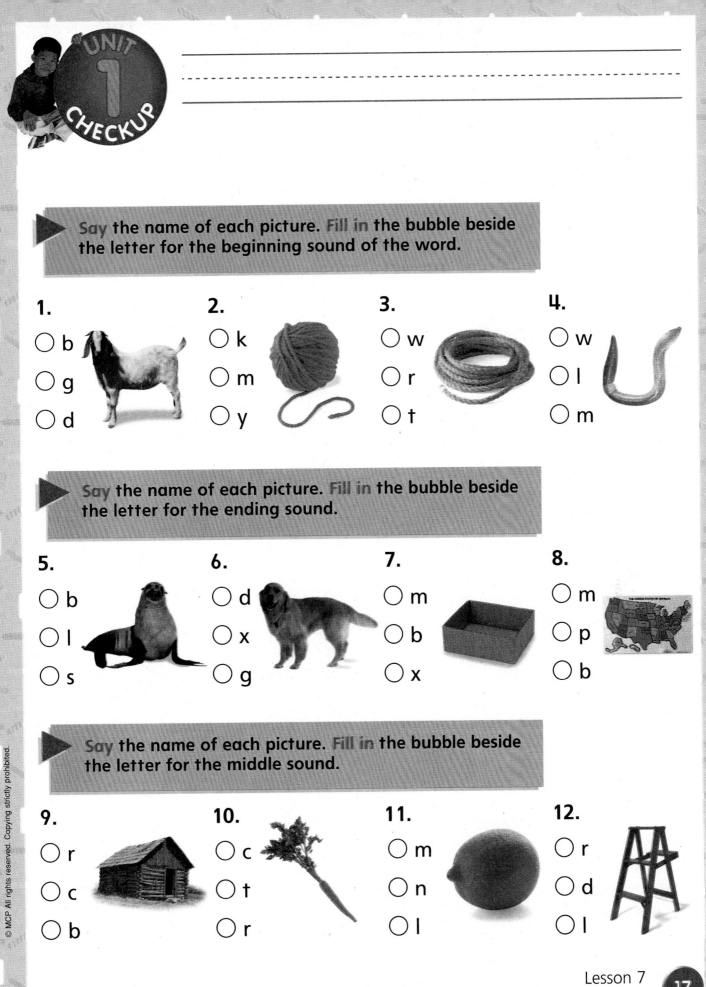

Circle the word that answers the riddle.
Print it on the line.

1. Jam goes in me. I am a _____ .

jar
car
farm

2. I rhyme with **drum.** I am _____ .

gas
gull
gum

3. A spider spins me. I am a _____ .

web
well
wet

4. I say "oink." I am a _____ .

big
pig
fig

5. I come after six. I am _____ .

seven
tiger
robot

6. I rhyme with **fox.** I am a _____ .

bag
box
bell

7. You can write with me. I am a _____ .

pet
peg
pen

8. You can ride in me. I am a _____ .

cabin
wagon
lemon

Lesson 7
Initial, medial, final consonants: Checkup

Home

With your child, take turns
making up riddles using the
words on the page.

Find the hidden pictures of things you can have fun with.

THINK! Which hidden thing would you want to play with most of all? Why?

Unit 2
Introduction
19

Home Letter

Dear Family,

Your child will want to share with you what we'll be doing in the next few weeks—learning to read and write words with these short vowel sounds.

a clap **e** bend **i** skip **o** hop **u** run

The names of many things that we do for fun contain short vowel sounds. In this unit, we will be learning about ways to have "fun in the sun."

At-Home Activities

Here are some simple, fun activities you and your child can do at home to practice short vowel sounds.

▶ Play a riddle game with your child. Think up a riddle whose answer is a short vowel word; for example: "I am what you do with a song. What am I?" (sing)

▶ Play "Concentration." Print words with short vowel sounds—two words for each sound—on individual cards or slips of paper. Shuffle the cards and place them face down. A player turns over two cards at a time. The object is to find two cards with the same vowel sound.

Book Corner

You and your child might enjoy reading these books together.

Almost Famous Daisy
by Richard Kidd
Daisy searches for inspiration when she enters the Famous Painting Contest.

Jo Jo's Flying Side Kick
by Brian Pinkney
Jo Jo demonstrates his strength and self-confidence as he tries to earn a yellow belt in his tae-kwon-do class.

Sincerely,

Fast, fast, fast.
My taxicab goes fast!
I can slow my cab down
As I get close to town.

RULE

If a word or syllable has only one vowel, and it comes at the beginning or between two consonants, the vowel is usually short. You can hear the short **a** sound in **fast.**

▶ **Circle the name of each picture.**

1

hat   ham

hand   had

2

bag   hat

bat   bad

3

camp   lad

lap   lamp

4

sad   back

bag   bat

5

cat   cap

cab   can

6

and   an

at   ant

7

mat   man

pan   map

8

cat   can

cab   cap

9

mad   ram

rack   mat

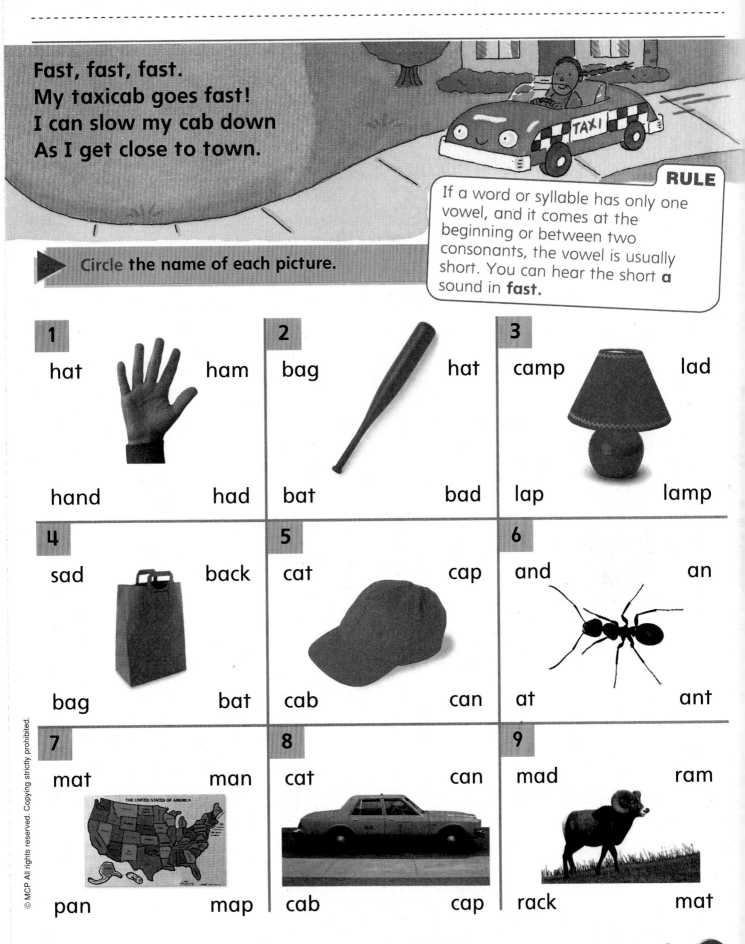

Draw a line through three words that rhyme in each box. Lines can go across, up and down, or on a diagonal.

1

ram	cab	gas
sad	ham	tag
bad	fan	yam

2

ax	lap	hat
wax	map	can
bag	nap	had

3

dad	tap	pal
bat	sat	cat
mat	pan	cap

4

tax	fat	tag
mad	wag	tab
bag	pad	sag

Lesson 8
Short vowel a: Phonograms

Home

Help your child think of another word to add to each group of rhyming words.

Find **words** in the box that rhyme with each child's name.
Print the rhyming words above or below each child's picture.

cat	ham	dad	fan	jam	van	hat	bad
sad	pan	yam	mat	can	bat	had	ram

1. Dan

2. Pat

3. Pam

4. Tad

1. I am Sam, and my cat is _____.   camp Pat cart

2. Pat likes milk and _____ food.   class sat cat

3. She eats a lot, but she is not _____.   van fat lamp

4. She likes to lick my _____.   hand gas band

5. Pat likes to sit on my _____.   lap ham Sam

6. Pat does not like to have a _____.   gap bath rack

7. She runs away as _____ as she can.   fast class bass

8. I _____ always find her.   can past fast

9. She takes a nap on a _____.   mast mat fat

10. She takes a _____ on Dad's lap.   ran sat nap

11. I _____ happy that Pat is my cat.   can am as

THINK! **Does the cat like Sam? How do you know?**

Home Ask your child to reread the sentences and name the short *a* words.

We will visit the city.
We will sit in the stands.
We will see the ball hit.
We will cheer with the fans.

> Circle **the name of each picture.**

1

sack
milk
mill
tap

2

mitt
fat
mat
mill

3

wind
tag
wig
wag

4

lap
lips
nap
dill

5

bag
pig
fig
pat

6

hill
bill
sill
hat

7

tax
six
fix
sat

8

bill
bit
hat
bib

9

wink
sank
sink
pink

Lesson 10
Short vowel i: Picture-text match

25

Color the parts of each ball with rhyming words the same color.

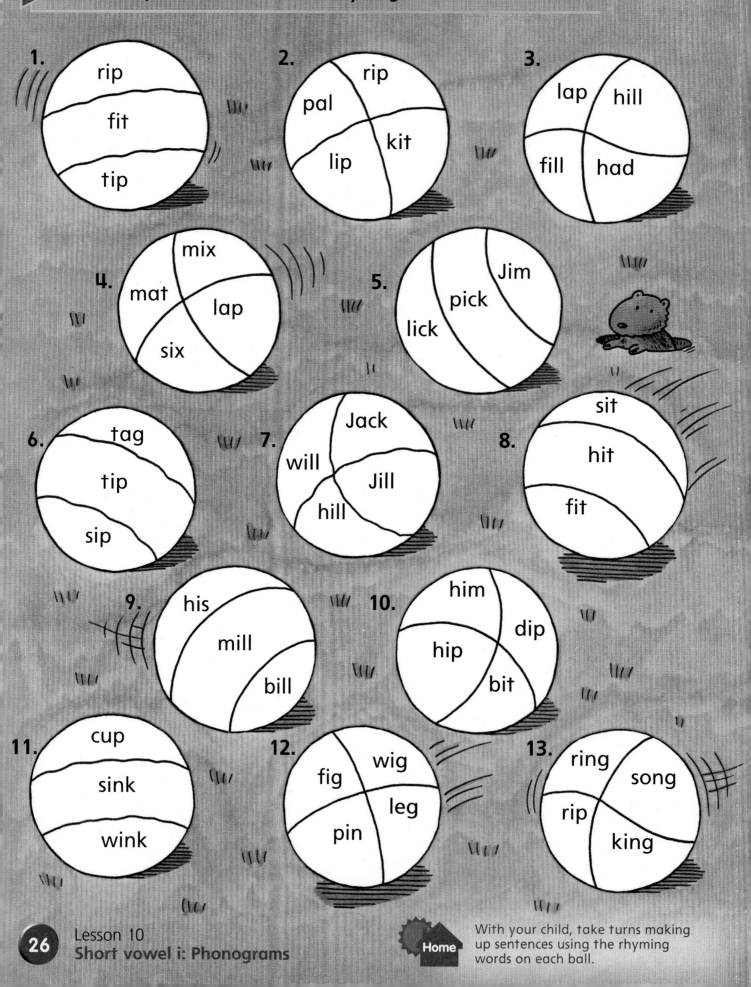

1. rip / fit / tip

2. rip / pal / kit / lip

3. lap / hill / fill / had

4. mix / mat / lap / six

5. Jim / pick / lick

6. tag / tip / sip

7. Jack / will / Jill / hill

8. sit / hit / fit

9. his / mill / bill

10. him / dip / hip / bit

11. cup / sink / wink

12. wig / fig / leg / pin

13. ring / song / rip / king

Lesson 10
Short vowel i: Phonograms

Home

With your child, take turns making up sentences using the rhyming words on each ball.

Print the word in the box that names each picture. In the last box, draw a picture of a short vowel word. Print the picture name.

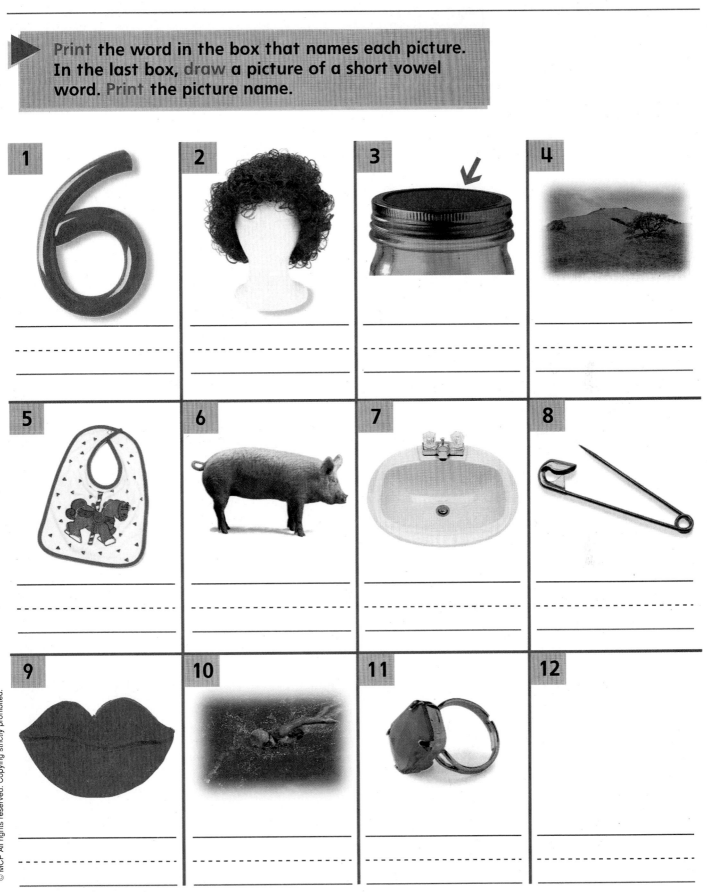

1

2

3

4

5

6

7

8

9

10

11

12

Lesson 11
Short vowel i: Spelling

27

Circle the word that answers each riddle. Print it on the line.

1 It can swim.
What is it?

_____

- - - - - - - - - - - -

_____

fast   fish

fix   fat

2 We drink it.
What is it?

_____

- - - - - - - - - - - -

_____

mitt   man

milk   mat

3 It comes after five.
What is it?

_____

- - - - - - - - - - - -

_____

sink   sad

sat   six

4 It rhymes with **bill.**
What is it?

_____

- - - - - - - - - - - -

_____

hit   hat

hill   ham

5 Lunch goes on it.
What is it?

_____

- - - - - - - - - - - -

_____

dad   dish

dig   did

6 It has a funny tail.
What is it?

_____

- - - - - - - - - - - -

_____

pin   pig

pal   pat

7 It fits on a finger.
What is it?

_____

- - - - - - - - - - - -

_____

rank   rat

rip   ring

8 A baby wears this.
What is it?

_____

- - - - - - - - - - - -

_____

bib   bad

bill   bat

9 I play ball with it.
What is it?

_____

- - - - - - - - - - - -

_____

mat   mitt

map   mix

Lesson 11
Short vowel i: Words in context

Ask your child to name a word that
rhymes with the answer to each riddle.

Circle the word that finishes each sentence. Print the word on the line.

1. We are going to take a _____. trap trip tan

2. Dad will look at the _____. map win cab

3. Pam will _____ the snacks. dish fix mix

4. We will _____ a tent. peck pack ram

5. Will our _____ fit in the van? sit big bags

6. My dog Wags can _____ with me. bat sit bib

7. Wait! Where is the _____? cat pat pick

Write a sentence to finish the story. Use some of the short a and short i words in the story.

Here's what to do.

1. Color the hills green.
2. Circle the pan.
3. Color the boy's cap black.
4. Draw a box around the ax.

5. Make an X on the man's hat.
6. Color the little fish blue.
7. Draw fins on the big fish.
8. Color the bag yellow.

Help your child list all the short *a* and short *i* words.

I can have fun,
Running in the sun.
Playing in the mud
With my friend Bud.

RULE

If a word or syllable has only one vowel, and it comes at the beginning or between two consonants, the vowel is usually short. You can hear the short **u** sound in **fun** and **mud**.

▶ Circle the name of each picture. Print the vowel you hear in the word you circled.

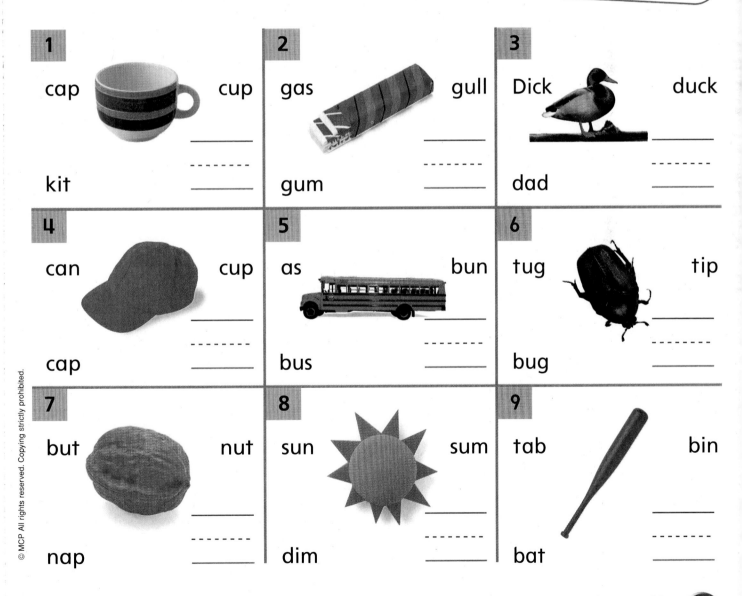

1
cap   cup

kit   _____

2
gas   gull

gum   _____

3
Dick   duck

dad   _____

4
can   cup

cap   _____

5
as   bun

bus   _____

6
tug   tip

bug   _____

7
but   nut

nap   _____

8
sun   sum

dim   _____

9
tab   bin

bat   _____

Find the word in the box that names each picture. **Print** it on the line.

bun	cup	rug	bus	bug	sun
gum	hug	hut	tub	jug	duck

1

2

3

4

5

6

7

8

9

10

11

12

Lesson 13
Short vowel u: Spelling

Home

Have your child make up silly sentences with words from the box that rhyme. Include other rhyming words.

Read the words in the box. Print a word in the puzzle to name each picture.

run bus tub
bun bug rug
cub sun nut

Across →

2.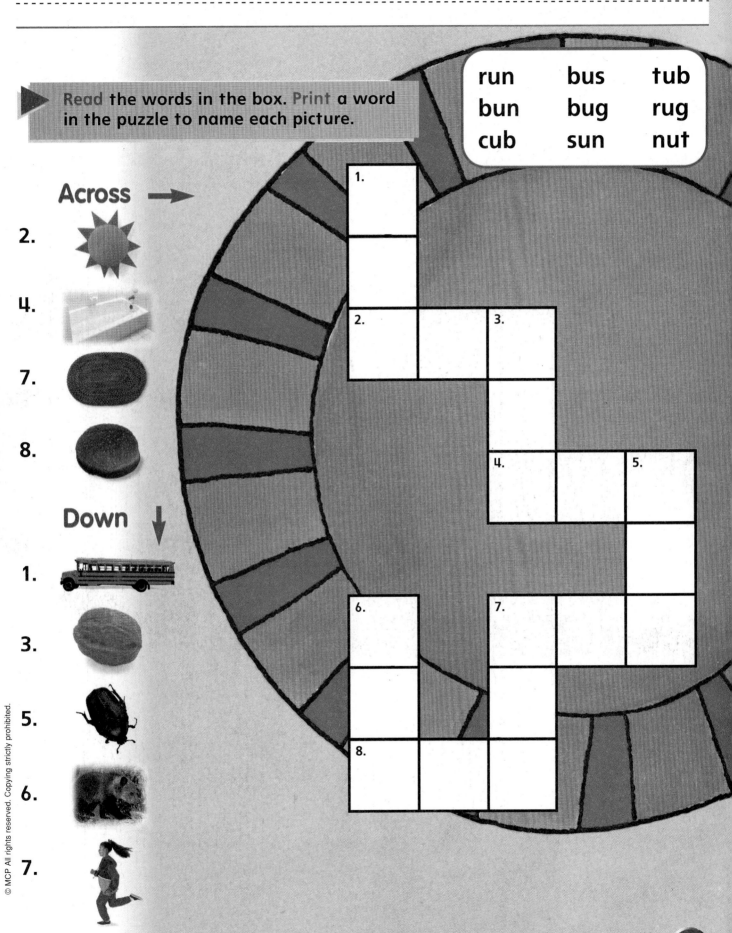

4.

7.

8.

Down ↓

1.

3.

5.

6.

7.

1. Today there was a fuss on the _____.

   _____
   run
   bus
   must

2. A _____ jumped on Gus.

   _____
   us
   bug
   hug

3. Gus jumped _____.

   _____
   run
   cup
   up

4. Then it jumped on _____.

   _____
   bus
   hug
   Russ

5. I saw the bug _____ on the window.

   _____
   just
   jump
   rust

6. It was _____ a little bug.

   _____
   just
   cup
   up

7. It liked to _____ up and down the window.

   _____
   rug
   run
   cup

8. The bug _____ like to ride on the bus.

   _____
   run
   us
   must

What would you do if you were on the bus?

Ask your child to spell the words he or she did not write in the sentences.

Read the story. Print a short **a**, **i**, or **u** word from the story to finish each sentence.

Ball Games

Balls are used in many different games. In some games, you hit the ball with a bat. Then you run fast! In other games, you jump up and hit the ball with your hand. In some games, you can hit the ball with anything but your hand! In yet another game, you can throw the ball, kick it, or run with it.

You can play ball games just about anywhere. You don't need much to have fun—just some friends and a ball!

1. You can hit a ball with a _____ or _____

   your _____.

2. When you hit the ball, you _____ fast!

3. In one game, you can throw the ball, run with it,

   or _____ it.

THINK! Name the games in the story.

Phonics & Writing

Write about a game you like to play. Don't give its name. Have your friends guess the game. Use these words and your own.

run jump

bat hit

cap kick

him fast

tag fun

Talk to your child about favorite games you played as a child.

Put it in the pot,
Shake it 'til it's hot.
Pop! Pop! Pop!
It's time to eat popcorn!

RULE
If a word or syllable has only one vowel, and it comes at the beginning or between two consonants, the vowel is usually short. You can hear the short **o** sound in **pop** and **hot**.

▶ **Find the word in the box that names each picture. Print it on the line.**

top	doll	lock	sock	hot	pot
Tom	pop	mop	box	rock	fox

1.

2.

3.

4.

5.

6.

7.

8.

9.

10.

11.

12.

Lesson 16
Short vowel o: Spelling

37

Circle the name of each picture.

1

fix
cob
fox
six

2

pot
top
tap
pit

3

bill
sill
dill
doll

4

fox
fix
box
bat

5

dog
dug
dig
pot

6

rock
sit
sack
sock

7

pig
pop
pup
pat

8

lag
log
bug
lot

9

luck
lock
lick
lack

10

mop
map
mud
milk

11

hat
hit
hot
hut

12

fix
tax
ax
ox

Lesson 16
Short vowel o: Picture-text match

Home

Have your child find the pictures on this page and on page 37 whose names rhyme.

_____

Help the frog hop to the pond. Look at each picture.
Write the name of each picture on the line.

top   dog   box   sock
lock   rock   log   fox   pot

**Fill in the bubble beside the sentence that tells about the picture.
Then draw a circle around each short o word in the sentences.**

1

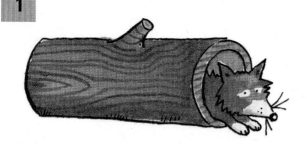

○ The fox is not on the log.
○ The fox is in the log.
○ The fox is on the log.
○ The fox is under the log.

2

○ Rob lost his sock.
○ Rob sat on a big rock.
○ Rob is on the big log.
○ Rob has a big rock in his hand.

3

○ The dog ran to the box.
○ The mop is not in the box.
○ I will hop on the log.
○ See the doll in the box.

4

○ I got the mop for Don.
○ Jill has the small top.
○ The small top is on the mop.
○ The top is in Bob's hand.

5

○ The hot pot is on the table.
○ Dot is not holding a hot pot.
○ Dot is holding a hot pot.
○ The milk in the pot is not hot.

Short vowel o: Words in context

Ask your child to read a
sentence that is not pictured,
and draw a picture for it.

Come on Fred and Jen,
Let's get wet!
It's a good way to cool off—
The best I've found yet!

Say the name of each picture. Print the name on the line.

RULE

If a word or syllable has only one vowel, and it comes at the beginning or between two consonants, the vowel is usually short. You can hear the short **e** sound in **get** and **wet.**

1

2

3

4

5

6

7

8

9

10

11

12

Print the name of each picture. Then do what the sentences tell you to do.

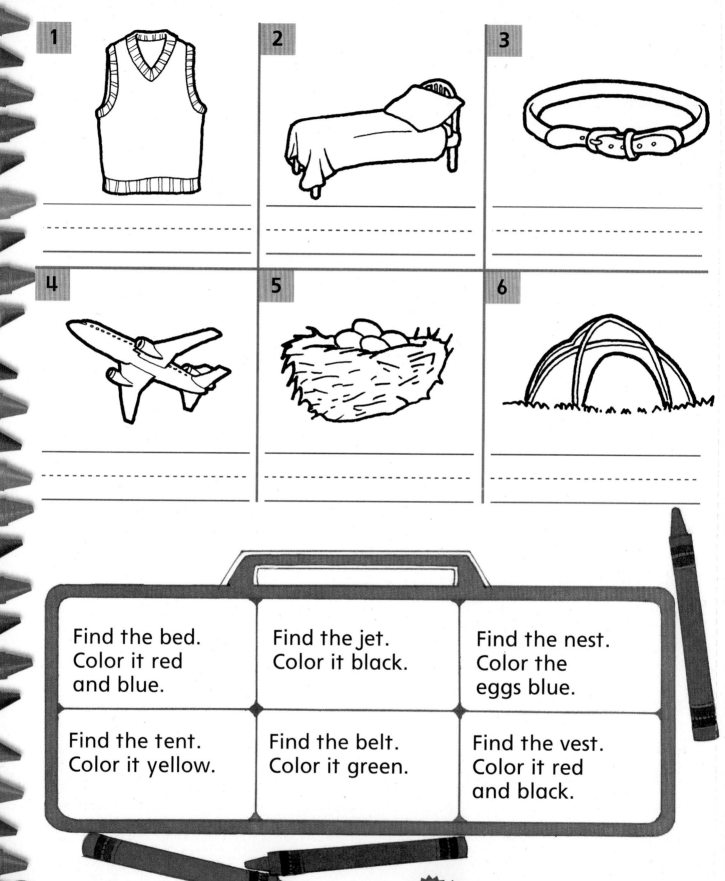

1

2

3

4

5

6

Find the bed.
Color it red
and blue.

Find the jet.
Color it black.

Find the nest.
Color the
eggs blue.

Find the tent.
Color it yellow.

Find the belt.
Color it green.

Find the vest.
Color it red
and black.

Lesson 18
Short vowel e: Spelling

 Home

Ask your child to find the names of
two colors on this page that have
the short e sound.

Fill in the bubble below the word that will finish each sentence. Print the word on the line.

1. My name is _____.

men   Jeff   jet
○   ○   ○

2. I want to get a _____.

bet   pet   yet
○   ○   ○

3. I would like a pet dog _____.

rest   west   best
○   ○   ○

4. I will _____ take care of my pet.

help   bell   nest
○   ○   ○

5. I can take it to the _____.

vet   bet   set
○   ○   ○

6. I will make sure it is _____.

get   fed   bed
○   ○   ○

7. It will need a good _____.

bed   nest   best
○   ○   ○

8. I will _____ it in and out.

jet   test   let
○   ○   ○

9. I can dry it when it's _____.

net   wet   set
○   ○   ○

10. I will _____ it if I get it.

sled   pet   west
○   ○   ○

11. I might name my pet _____.

Pepper   fed   set
○   ○   ○

12. I will _____ Ned about my pet.

sell   tell   fell
○   ○   ○

THINK!

Why would Jeff make a good pet owner?

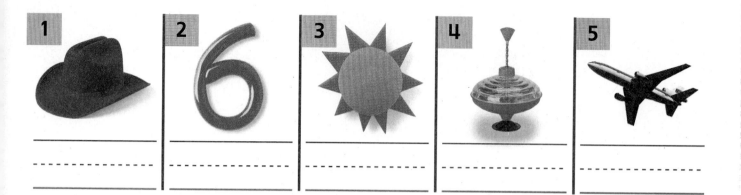

1	2	3	4	5

▶ **Print** yes **or** no **on the line to answer each question.**

6. You can sit in a tent.

7. A hen can lay eggs.

8. A cat has six legs.

9. A big bus can jump up and down.

10. You can go fast in a jet.

11. An ant is as big as an ox.

12. Six is less than ten.

13. You can rest in a bed.

14. You have ten fingers and ten toes.

 Home Ask your child to circle and read the short e words in each sentence.

Say and spell each short vowel word. Print the word on the banner of the plane that shows its short vowel sound.

Word List

net	wig	ox	cab	bun
ram	nut	doll	leg	dish
lips	web	ax	sun	box

Short a

Short e

Short i

Short o

Short u

Phonics & Writing

dig	fun	swim	hot	camp
run	net	doll	sand	pet

TO:
My Friend
2 Blue Lane
Yourtown, USA
12345

Book Corner

A Lot Happened Today
by Judy Nayer

When Jared's teacher gives him a journal, he records his starring role in a baseball game.

 Home

Ask your child to name the words on the postcard that have short vowel sounds.

6

8

Sticky Tag

When you
tag someone,
he becomes
It and must
keep
his hand on
the spot
you tagged.

Can you
make up
another kind
of tag that is
fun to play?

TALK ABOUT IT

— FOLD —

FOLD

3

Chain Tag

When you tag someone, she links arms
with you. Then both of you chase the
rest. Everyone you tag joins the chain!

1

This book belongs to

Twists on Tag

Flashlight Tag

Had enough fun in the sun? Play tag in the dark. Just hit someone with a flash of light and yell, "Tag, you're It!"

7

FOLD

Shadow Tag

You need to have sun for this twist on tag. To tag someone, you must step on her shadow!

5

FOLD

Tag is fun to play. But just plain tag can get boring fast. Here are some twists to make the fun of tag last.

2

Rainbow Tag

When you become It, you name a color. You can only tag children who are wearing that color.

4

Fill in the bubble beside the name of each picture.

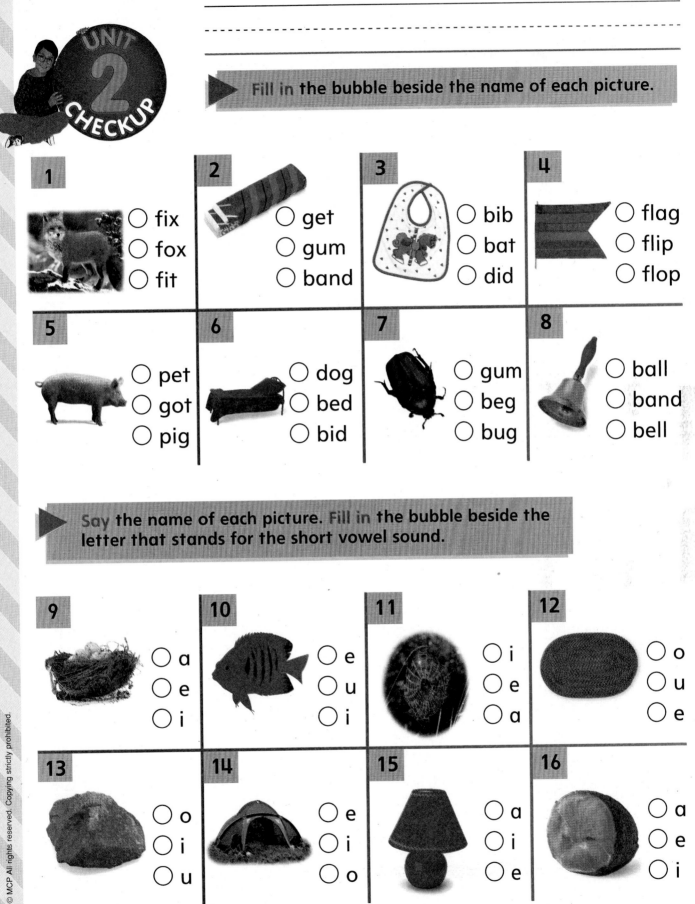

1
- ○ fix
- ○ fox
- ○ fit

2
- ○ get
- ○ gum
- ○ band

3
- ○ bib
- ○ bat
- ○ did

4
- ○ flag
- ○ flip
- ○ flop

5
- ○ pet
- ○ got
- ○ pig

6
- ○ dog
- ○ bed
- ○ bid

7
- ○ gum
- ○ beg
- ○ bug

8
- ○ ball
- ○ band
- ○ bell

Say the name of each picture. Fill in the bubble beside the letter that stands for the short vowel sound.

9
- ○ a
- ○ e
- ○ i

10
- ○ e
- ○ u
- ○ i

11
- ○ i
- ○ e
- ○ a

12
- ○ o
- ○ u
- ○ e

13
- ○ o
- ○ i
- ○ u

14
- ○ e
- ○ i
- ○ o

15
- ○ a
- ○ i
- ○ e

16
- ○ a
- ○ e
- ○ i

Find the word in the box that will finish each sentence. Print the word on the line.

1. After the rain, the _____ came out.

2. I _____ out to play and have fun.

3. I slid in the _____ mud.

4. I _____ and landed with a thud!

5. Then I was covered with _____.

6. Mom said I _____ to come in.

| ran |
| mud |
| sun |
| wet |
| had |
| fell |

7. I got mud on the _____.

8. Mom was not _____.

9. She made me _____ in the tub.

10. Then she gave me a glass of _____.

11. Now it was time to go to _____.

12. I did not mind because I had _____.

| bed |
| fun |
| hop |
| mad |
| milk |
| rug |

Read Aloud

I Like to Go Places

I like to go places,
There is so much to see.
I'll travel the open road
Or sail the deep blue sea.

I'll row in a rowboat
Or ride in a jet plane.
Put me in a sailboat,
And I won't complain.

I'll even ride a mean old mule
Or sit in a big blue jeep.
And if I have to take a hike,
I'll use my own two feet!

There are so many places to go,
And so many people to meet.

► **Name some different ways to travel.**

**How would you travel
to faraway places?**

Unit 3
Introduction

51

Home Letter

Dear Family,

As we explore different ways of traveling and places to visit, your child will be learning long vowel sounds in words like boat, jeep, bike, plane, and mule.

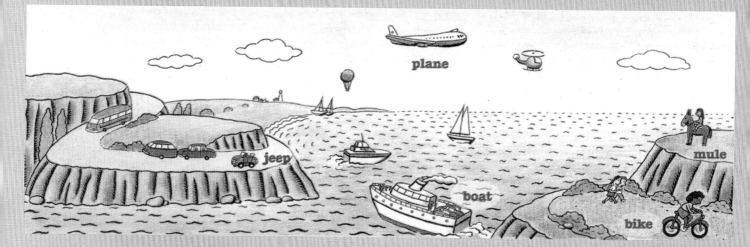

At-Home Activities

Here are some activities you and your child can do together.

▶ Read a travel brochure (or advertisement in the travel section of the newspaper) about a place you would like to visit. Help your child pick out words with long vowel sounds.

▶ Ask your child to write about a trip he or she would like to take. Encourage your child to draw a picture to go with the story. Talk about the story and then take turns pointing to all the words with long vowels.

Book Corner

You and your child might enjoy reading these books together. Look for them in your local library.

My Sister's Rusty Bike
by Jim Aylesworth

A young narrator takes a humorous tour across America on his sister's rusty bicycle.

The Train to Lulu's
by Elizabeth Howard

Two sisters set out on a special adventure—traveling by train from Boston to Baltimore in the 1950s.

Sincerely,

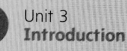

Let's play up and away.
You be the tail and do as I say:
Wave your arms wide, dip and sway.
We're like a plane that's on its way!

RULE

If a word or syllable has two vowels, the first vowel usually stands for the long sound, and the second vowel is silent. You can hear the long **a** sound in **wave, plane,** and **play.**

▶ **Find the word that will finish each sentence. Print it on the line.**

1. Jane made a _____ when she saw it rain.

2. She wanted the rain to go _____.

3. She had planned to _____ outside.

4. Then Jake _____ over.

5. Jake and Jane played _____ inside.

away
face
games
came
play

6. The children had to _____ for the rain to stop.

7. Jane's sister baked a _____.

8. Jane and Jake _____ a piece.

9. At last the _____ stopped.

rain
ate
wait
cake

THINK! **What could Jane and Jake do outside?**

Circle **each long a** word in the box.
Then print **the name of each picture on the line.**

tap	tape	cap	cape	at	ate
mail	mat	rain	gate	hay	ham

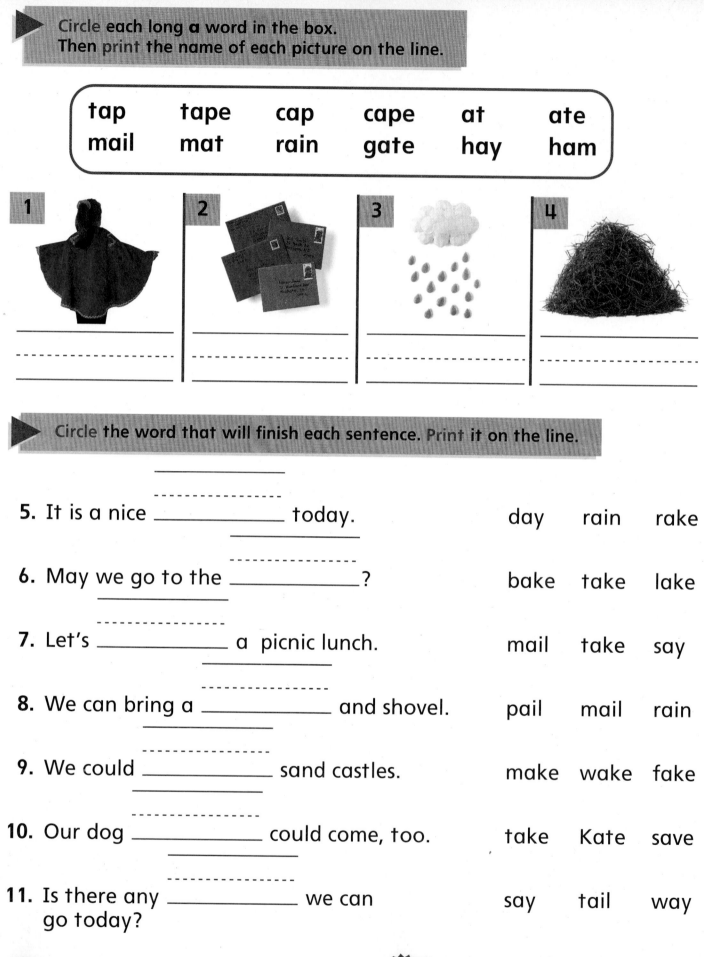

1

2

3

4

_____
- - - - - - - - - - - - - - - -
_____

Circle **the word that will finish each sentence. Print it on the line.**

_____
- - - - - - - - - - - - - - -

5. It is a nice _____ today.   day   rain   rake

_____
- - - - - - - - - - - - - - -

6. May we go to the _____?   bake   take   lake

_____
- - - - - - - - - - - - - - -

7. Let's _____ a picnic lunch.   mail   take   say

_____
- - - - - - - - - - - - - - -

8. We can bring a _____ and shovel.   pail   mail   rain

_____
- - - - - - - - - - - - - - -

9. We could _____ sand castles.   make   wake   fake

_____
- - - - - - - - - - - - - - -

10. Our dog _____ could come, too.   take   Kate   save

_____
- - - - - - - - - - - - - - -

11. Is there any _____ we can   say   tail   way
go today?

Lesson 23
Long vowel a

Home

Ask your child to reread the
sentences on page 53. Identify
the long _a_ words.

Tie a line to your kite.
Tie the kite to your bike.
Ride as fast as you can
And your kite will take flight.

RULE

If a word or syllable has two vowels, the first vowel usually stands for the long sound, and the second vowel is silent. You can hear the long **i** sound in **line** and **kite**.

> Circle **the name of each picture.**

1

dim   dime

2

pig   pile

3

bike   bib

4

bib   bite

> Circle **the word that will finish each sentence. Then print it on the line.**

5. Mike likes to ride a _____.   bit   bike   bite

6. Diane likes to _____.   hike   hill   him

7. Ike likes cherry _____.   pie   pig   pine

8. Kyle likes to fly a _____.   bite   hive   kite

9. Fido likes to _____.   rid   hide   hive

10. We all like lunch _____.   tide   time   tip

▶ **Circle** the word that will finish each sentence. **Print** it on the line.

1. A turtle can _____ inside its shell.   dime time hide

2. A _____ can hide in a den very well.   lion tile pie

3. My dog can hide behind our _____.   likes bikes dives

4. A bee can hide in its _____.   hive time kite

5. A spider can hide anywhere it _____.   pine mine likes

6. I _____ to hide things here and there.   like mile dime

7. No one can _____ them anywhere.   kind find pile

▶ **Circle** each long **i** word in the box.
Print the name of each picture on the line.

| dim | dime | pin | pine | rid | ride |
| mine | tie | sit | kite | nine | line |

8 _____ 9 _____ 10 _____ 11 _____

_____

- -

_____

> **Read** each riddle. **Circle** the word that answers the riddle. **Print** it on the line.

1. This can fly.   rake   kite   kit

2. A dog can wag it.   tail   tie   pat

3. We did it to a cake.   at   time   ate

4. Jane has a can of it.   pat   pant   paint

5. We ride boats on this.   bat   mile   lake

6. We like to eat it.   bit   pie   pat

7. We can ride it.   bill   bat   bike

8. We do this to shoes.   tip   tie   time

9. We can save this.   like   dime   dip

10. A wet day has this.   rain   rake   ran

11. We play this.   bat   gate   game

12. A clock tells this.   time   Tim   take

Read the words in the balloons. **Print** the long **a** words under Kay's name. **Print** the long **i** words under Mike's name.

pan

tail

sail

lid

bake

pat

kite

pin

bike

like

lake

ride

rake

side

cake

dime

Kay

Mike

Lesson 25
Review long vowels a, i

Home

Have your child suggest one or more additional long *a* or long *i* words.

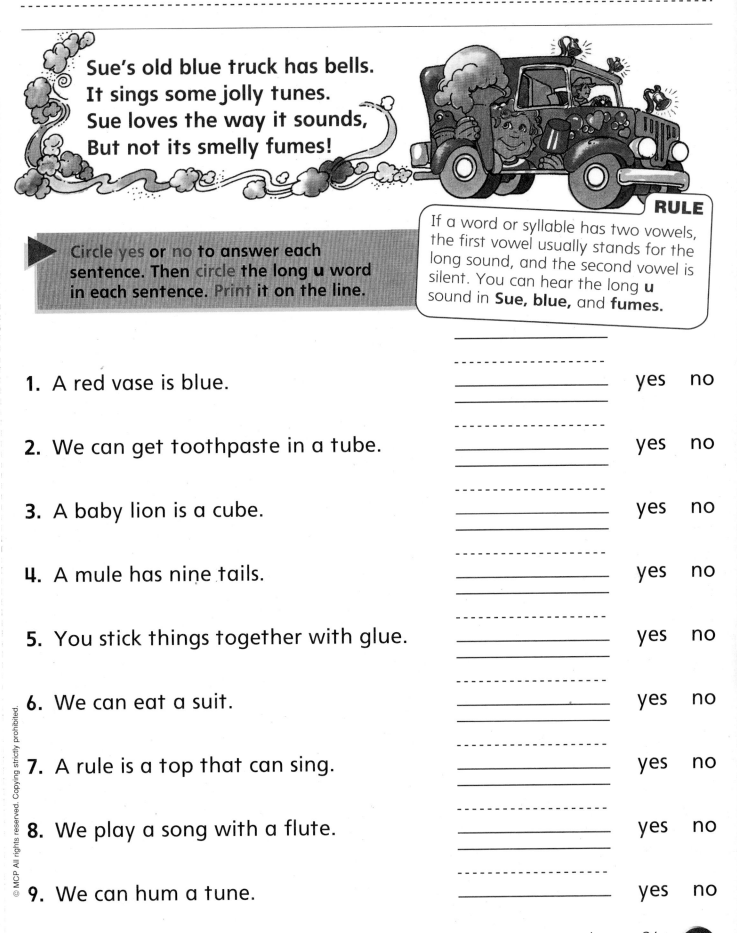

Sue's old blue truck has bells.
It sings some jolly tunes.
Sue loves the way it sounds,
But not its smelly fumes!

RULE

If a word or syllable has two vowels, the first vowel usually stands for the long sound, and the second vowel is silent. You can hear the long **u** sound in **Sue**, **blue**, and **fumes**.

▶ Circle yes **or** no to answer each sentence. Then circle the long **u** word in each sentence. Print it on the line.

1. A red vase is blue. _____ yes   no

2. We can get toothpaste in a tube. _____ yes   no

3. A baby lion is a cube. _____ yes   no

4. A mule has nine tails. _____ yes   no

5. You stick things together with glue. _____ yes   no

6. We can eat a suit. _____ yes   no

7. A rule is a top that can sing. _____ yes   no

8. We play a song with a flute. _____ yes   no

9. We can hum a tune. _____ yes   no

Read the words in the box. Print the short u words in the ducks' pond. Print the long u words in the mule's pen.

bug	jump	suit	tune	bump	tube
dug	glue	nut	rule	use	hum
	luck	jug	blue	flute	

short

long

Lesson 26
Long vowel u

Home

Ask your child to suggest a short *u* name for the duck and a long *u* name for the mule.

1 late ○ long ○ short

2 June ○ long ○ short

3 mule ○ long ○ short

4 man ○ long ○ short

5 tube ○ long ○ short

6 ride ○ long ○ short

7 rain ○ long ○ short

8 pick ○ long ○ short

9 six ○ long ○ short

10 use ○ long ○ short

11 cute ○ long ○ short

12 cap ○ long ○ short

13 bat ○ long ○ short

14 time ○ long ○ short

15 fun ○ long ○ short

16 bake ○ long ○ short

17 lick ○ long ○ short

18 us ○ long ○ short

19 map ○ long ○ short

20 wide ○ long ○ short

21 gate ○ long ○ short

22 wipe ○ long ○ short

23 pie ○ long ○ short

24 tune ○ long ○ short

Circle the word that will finish each sentence. Print it on the line.

1. We _____ to play music.　　ride　like　hike

2. It is a nice _____ to spend a day.　　pay　side　way

3. June likes to play her _____.　　flute　suit　time

4. Jay can play his _____.　　bake　tuba　tub

5. Mike _____ tunes on his bugle.　　side　skit　plays

6. Sue plays a _____, too.　　bugle　suit　like

7. _____ like to play my drum.　　It　I　Ice

8. We all sing _____.　　tunes　times　tiles

9. We can play _____ in a parade.　　music　suit　fan

10. Will our uniforms come on _____?　　tip　cub　time

11. We play at a football _____, too!　　gum　game　gate

THINK! What kind of group do the children belong to?

Lesson 27
Review long vowels a, i, u

Home

Ask your child to group the words he or she wrote according to the vowel sound.

Playing for the President

Julie plays the tuba in her school band. Her friend Dave plays the flute. They are very excited. They are going to the White House to play for the President.

Washington, D.C. is far away from home so they take the train. They spend the time playing games. The next day they arrive at the station.

At the White House everyone waits. When the President comes out, Julie takes a deep breath and begins to play. The President smiles. He likes their music. When he leaves he hums a tune.

1. The band rides in a _____ to Washington, D.C.

2. Julie plays the _____, and Dave

   plays the _____.

3. The President _____ their _____.

How do you know it was a long train ride?

Phonics & Writing

Write about a trip you have taken with your class. Where did you go? How did you get there? What did you see? Use some of the words in the box.

train	bike	sail	blue
use	away	lake	hike
time	like	ride	day

Lesson 28
Review long a, i, u: Writing

Ask your child to spell the words in the box.

I know a silly mole
in a yellow overcoat.
He rows down the coast
in a little silver boat.

I hope to go with Mole
to places near and far.
If we can't go by boat,
then we'll go by car.

> **Find the word in the box that will finish each sentence. Print it on the line.**

RULE

If a word or syllable has two vowels, the first vowel usually stands for the long sound, and the second vowel is silent. You can hear the long **o** sound in **know, mole,** and **boat.**

coat
owner
Rover
show
bowl
bone
nose

1. Rover poked his _____ into his bowl.

2. He hoped to find a _____.

3. There was no bone in his _____.

4. Then along came his _____, Joe.

5. Something was in the pocket of Joe's _____.

6. Joe said, "I have something to _____ you."

7. Oh, boy! It was a bone for _____.

THINK! **What do dogs like to do with bones?**

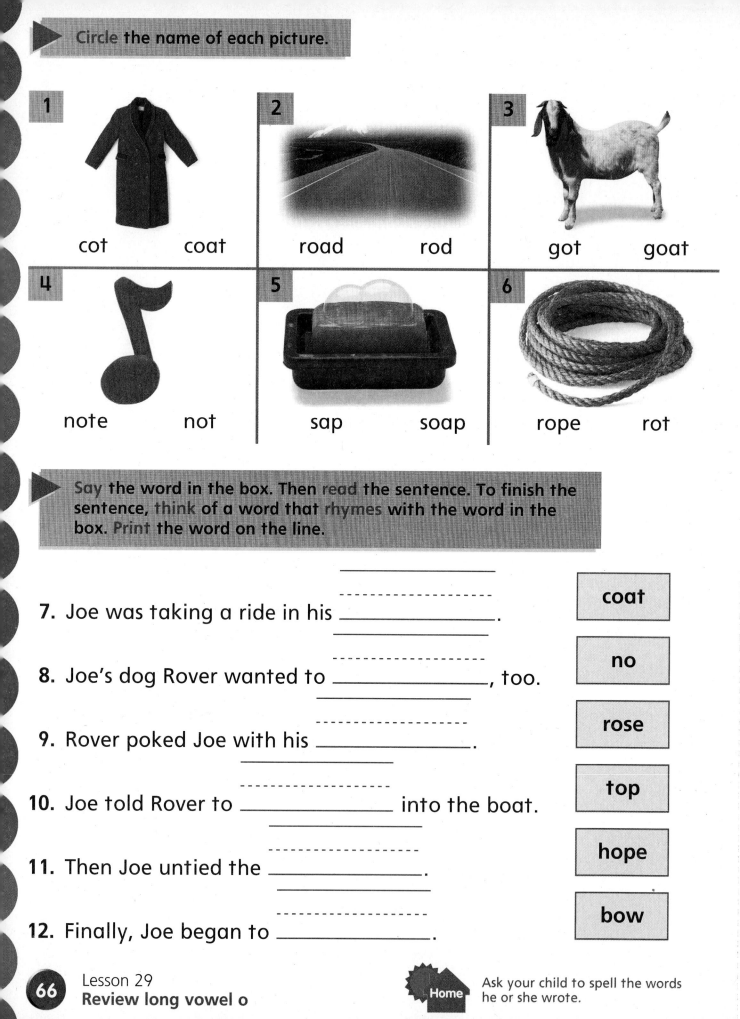

Circle the name of each picture.

1
cot   coat

2
road   rod

3
got   goat

4
note   not

5
sap   soap

6
rope   rot

Say the word in the box. Then **read** the sentence. To finish the sentence, **think** of a word that **rhymes** with the word in the box. **Print** the word on the line.

7. Joe was taking a ride in his _____.

8. Joe's dog Rover wanted to _____, too.

9. Rover poked Joe with his _____.

10. Joe told Rover to _____ into the boat.

11. Then Joe untied the _____.

12. Finally, Joe began to _____.

coat

no

rose

top

hope

bow

Lesson 29
Review long vowel o

Home

Ask your child to spell the words he or she wrote.

Print the name of each picture on the line.

1.

2.

3.

4.

5.

6.

What would you pack if you were taking a trip? Choose a word from the suitcase that rhymes and print it on the line.

7. Very nice! Pack some toy _____.

8. Oh, my! Don't forget your _____.

9. How cute! Take your bathing _____.

10. For goodness' sake! Bring a little _____.

tie
mice
suit
rake

1. Tim had a nice _____ outside. ○ Tim ○ time

2. He _____ his bike. ○ rode ○ rod

3. He flew his _____ with June. ○ kite ○ kit

4. He played _____ and seek. ○ hid ○ hide

5. Then _____ and June came inside. ○ Tim ○ time

6. They _____ some cookies. ○ mad ○ made

7. They _____ every single bite. ○ ate ○ at

8. "Let's make ice _____," said June. ○ cubes ○ cub

9. "We can _____ grape juice." ○ us ○ use

10. Next Tim made a paper _____. ○ plan ○ plane

11. June made a paper _____. ○ hate ○ hat

12. Tim said, "I _____ you had fun." ○ hope ○ hop

THINK! Do you think Tim and June had fun? Why or why not?

Home Ask your child to read the sentences and identify which words have long vowel sounds.

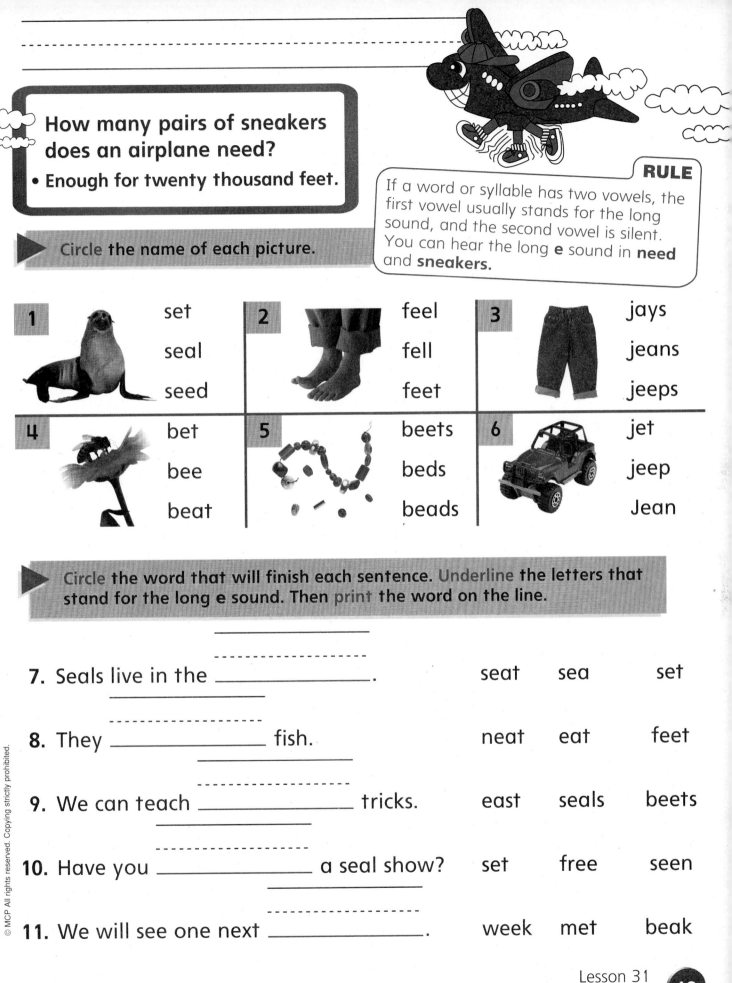

How many pairs of sneakers does an airplane need?
• Enough for twenty thousand feet.

▶ Circle the name of each picture.

1 set / seal / seed

2 feel / fell / feet

3 jays / jeans / jeeps

4 bet / bee / beat

5 beets / beds / beads

6 jet / jeep / Jean

▶ Circle the word that will finish each sentence. Underline the letters that stand for the long **e** sound. Then print the word on the line.

7. Seals live in the _____. seat   sea   set

8. They _____ fish. neat   eat   feet

9. We can teach _____ tricks. east   seals   beets

10. Have you _____ a seal show? set   free   seen

11. We will see one next _____. week   met   beak

Lesson 31
Long vowel e   69

Circle the long e words in the puzzle.

k	f	s	r	j
s	e	e	n	e
a	e	a	o	a
s	t	t	p	n
p	e	a	b	s

jeans

feet

pea

seat

seen

Write the word from the box that will finish each sentence.

1. I wore my new blue _____ to the zoo.

2. I sat on a _____ that had gum on it.

3. I spilled _____ soup on my jeans.

4. Mud from my _____ splashed on them.

5. I've never _____ such a big mess.

Ask your child to read the answers and tell what letters stand for the long e sound.

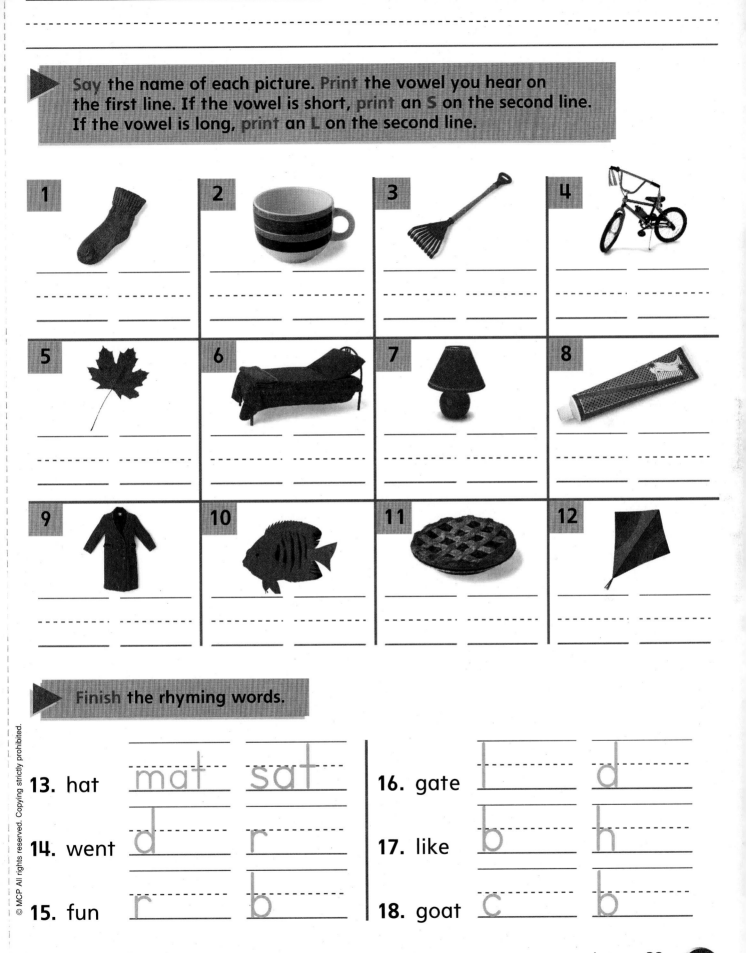

Say the name of each picture. Print the vowel you hear on the first line. If the vowel is short, print an **S** on the second line. If the vowel is long, print an **L** on the second line.

Finish the rhyming words.

13. hat   mat   sat

14. went   d_____   r_____

15. fun   r_____   b_____

16. gate   l_____   d_____

17. like   b_____   h_____

18. goat   c_____   b_____

Change the first vowel in each word to make a new word.

1. boat _____

2. sod _____

3. red _____

4. oar _____

5. hop _____

6. ran _____

7. cone _____

8. wide _____

9. bake _____

10. nip _____

11. tame _____

12. map _____

Find a word in the box that rhymes with each word. Print it on the line.

13. time _____

14. cube _____

15. rub _____

16. need _____

17. tape _____

18. bat _____

19. clue _____

| tube |
| cub |
| blue |
| cape |
| dime |
| hat |
| feed |

20. seat _____

21. fin _____

22. hope _____

23. bet _____

24. rob _____

25. toad _____

26. fine _____

| tin |
| road |
| cob |
| mine |
| rope |
| get |
| heat |

72 Lesson 32
Review long and short vowels

Home

Ask your child to read the rhyming words and tell whether each pair has a long or short vowel sound.

Phonics & Spelling

Say and spell each long vowel word. Print the word on the train that shows its long vowel sound.

Word List

use	heel	hay	nine	note
coat	tube	dime	rule	bead
cape	tie	seen	mail	row

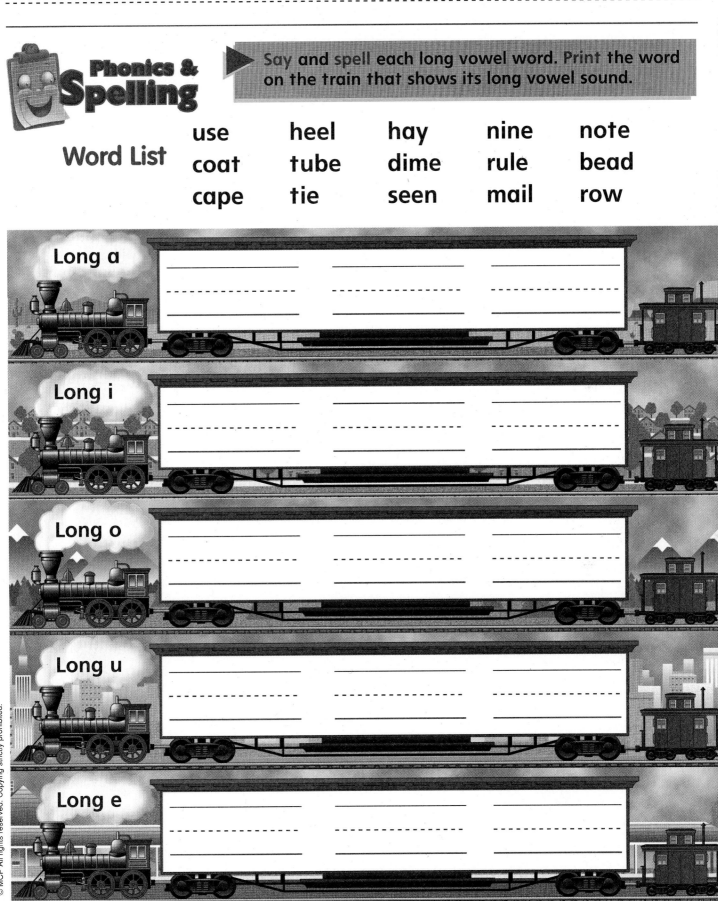

Long a

Long i

Long o

Long u

Long e

▶ Write about a place you have visited or would like to visit. Use some of the words in the box.

blue	boat	hay	hole	seat
mail	jeans	hope	train	row
bike	ride	use	time	rain

Book Corner

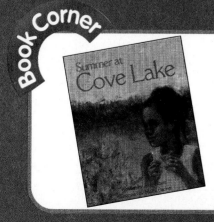

Summer at Cove Lake
by Judy Lechner

A young girl finds many new things when she spends the summer with her aunt.

8

What special place would you like to see? How would you get there?

TALK ABOUT IT

6

Do you like animals? Then the San Diego Zoo in California is the place for you.

FOLD

FOLD

3

Climb up high. You can see the whole city. Everything looks tiny from way up here.

1

This book belongs to:

So Many Sights to see

Take the zoo train to see the lions, tigers, zebras, and apes. Don't forget the seals!

7

From the plane you can see people riding mules down a steep path.

5

FOLD

FOLD

There are so many exciting places to see. You can take a boat to the Statue of Liberty in New York.

2

You can fly over the Grand Canyon in Arizona. It is very wide and very deep.

4

Lesson 34
Review long vowels: Take-Home Book

Say the name of each picture. Print the vowel you hear on the line. Then circle the word short if the vowel is short. Circle the word long if it is long.

1
_____ long
_____ short

2
_____ long
_____ short

3
_____ long
_____ short

4
_____ long
_____ short

5
_____ long
_____ short

6
_____ long
_____ short

7
_____ long
_____ short

8
_____ long
_____ short

9
_____ long
_____ short

10
_____ long
_____ short

11
_____ long
_____ short

12
_____ long
_____ short

13
_____ long
_____ short

14
_____ long
_____ short

15
_____ long
_____ short

16
_____ long
_____ short

Lesson 35
Long and short vowels: Checkup

 77

Fill in the bubble in front of the word that will finish each sentence.

1. I have a ___ named Wags.　　○ fog　　○ dog　　○ day

2. His ___ always wags.　　○ tap　　○ tape　　○ tail

3. Wags is a very ___ dog.　　○ cute　　○ cut　　○ cat

4. He ___ food by the bags.　　○ eats　　○ ears　　○ east

5. His tummy is ___ and sags.　　○ bite　　○ big　　○ kite

6. His long ears flap ___ flags.　　○ like　　○ lime　　○ lit

7. Wags and I like to ___.　　○ fat　　○ way　　○ play

8. We like to ___ walks, too.　　○ take　　○ tack　　○ tail

9. I ___ him to go one way.　　○ fell　　○ tell　　○ bean

10. He always ___ the other way.　　○ toes　　○ got　　○ goes

11. But he would never ___ away.　　○ fun　　○ run　　○ use

12. A dog like Wags is a ___ of fun.　　○ lot　　○ lock　　○ low

78 Lesson 35
Long and short vowels: Checkup

▶ **What is wrong with this picture?**

What do you think a scarecrow does in the garden?

Home Letter

Dear Family,

In the next few weeks we'll be learning about different kinds of words and sounds: compounds (scarecrow), consonant blends (**gr**apes), digraphs (pea**ch**, **wh**eat), r-controlled vowels (c**or**n), and **y** as a vowel (cherr**y**). We will also be learning about nature and the world outside.

scarecrow **grapes** **peach** **wheat** **corn** **cherry**

At-Home Activities

Here are some activities you and your child can do together.

▶ Plant a bean or some grass seed in a paper cup. Talk about what seeds need to grow.

▶ Write the following words on separate pieces of paper: sail, boat, pop, corn, mail, box, note, and book. Take turns pairing the words to make compound words. Make a list of compound words with your child and add to it as you think of new words.

Book Corner

You and your child might enjoy reading these books together.

Potato
by Barrie Watts

Children learn about potato plants and how edible parts grow underground.

Alphabet Garden
by Laura Jane Coats

Children take an alphabetical tour of a garden.

Sincerely,

Name _____

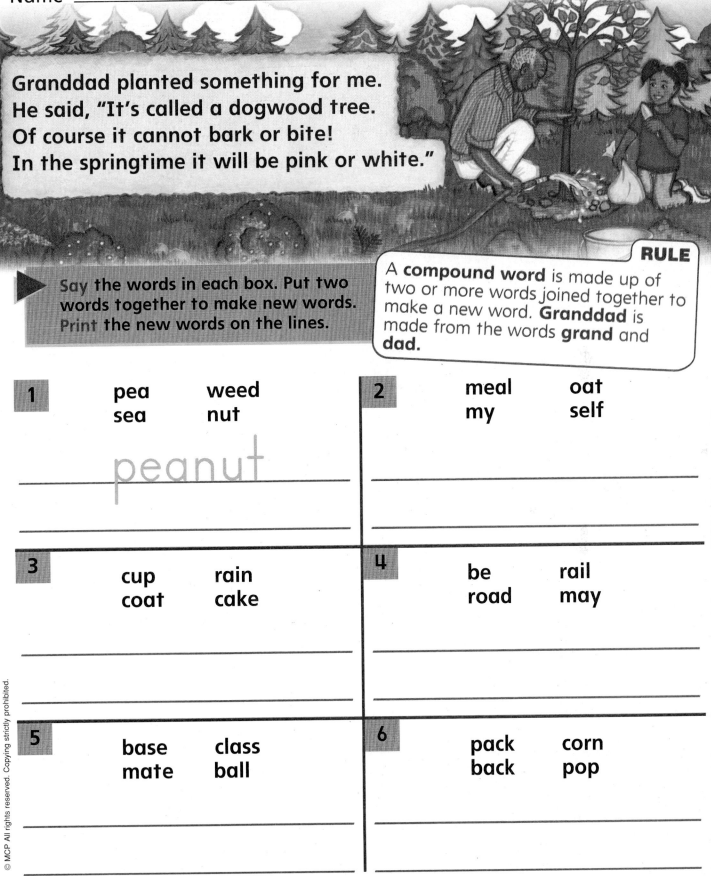

Granddad planted something for me.
He said, "It's called a dogwood tree.
Of course it cannot bark or bite!
In the springtime it will be pink or white."

► Say the words in each box. Put two words together to make new words. Print the new words on the lines.

RULE

A **compound word** is made up of two or more words joined together to make a new word. **Granddad** is made from the words **grand** and **dad.**

1

pea	weed
sea	nut

peanut
_____

_____

2

meal	oat
my	self

_____

_____

3

cup	rain
coat	cake

_____

_____

4

be	rail
road	may

_____

_____

5

base	class
mate	ball

_____

_____

6

pack	corn
back	pop

_____

_____

1. mail + box   A box for mail is a _____.

2. rain + coat   A coat for rain is a _____.

3. back + pack   A pack for your back is a _____.

4. sail + boat   A boat with a sail is a _____.

5. pop + corn   Corn that can pop is _____.

6. sand + box   A box full of sand is a _____.

7. cup + cake   A cake in a cup is a _____.

Lesson 36
Compound Words: Words in context

Home

Help your child think of other compound words and draw pictures of each one.

Name _____

Farmer Janet picks some carrots.
She picks a turnip, too.
She'll take these to her cabin
And make a farmer's stew.

> Say the name of each picture. Circle each vowel you hear. Print the number of syllables you hear on the line.

Many words are made of small parts called syllables. Each syllable has one vowel sound.
p(i)cks = 1 syllable c(a)rr(o)ts = 2 syllables

1	b(a)sk(e)t
2	mittens
3	steps
4	pencil
5	tent
6	puppet
7	trunk
8	robot
9	pillow
10	kitten
11	tray
12	lemon

**Find the word in the box that names each picture.
Print it on the line to finish the sentence.**

ribbon	basket	button	pillow
kitten	boxes	seven	baby

1. Molly got a _____ named Popcorn.

2. She put a _____ in Popcorn's fur.

3. Popcorn was only _____ weeks old.

4. She had a nose like a _____.

5. She liked to play inside _____.

6. Molly made a bed for Popcorn in a _____.

7. She put a _____ in the bed to make it soft.

8. Popcorn was like a little _____.

THINK! **Why is Popcorn like a baby?**

Lesson 37
Two-syllable words: Words in context

Home

Say one- and two-syllable words
and have your child identify the
number of syllables.

Name _____

Pick a bag of apples.
Pick a basket of cucumbers, too.
There's some applesauce
on the table,
And a dill pickle just for you.

▶ Find the name of each picture in the box. Print it on the line.

apple	eagle	people
candle	buckle	whistle
turtle	bottle	table

1 _____

2 _____

3 _____

4 _____

5 _____

6 _____

7 _____

8 _____

9 _____

Lesson 38
Words ending in le: Picture-text match

1. A _____ uses its own shell for a house.

2. It can swim in a small _____.

3. It can _____ around in the puddle.

4. It climbs on rocks and _____.

5. An _____ might fly over and scare it.

6. Sometimes, _____ may scare it, too.

7. Then the turtle can _____ safely in its shell.

> pebbles
> eagle
> people
> turtle
> huddle
> puddle
> paddle

8. I have a _____ pet turtle.

9. My _____ gave it to me.

10. It's not even as big as a _____.

11. I named my turtle _____.

12. When I hold it, its feet _____ my hand.

13. Then I laugh and _____.

14. Sometimes, it sits on the _____ next to my bed.

> giggle
> table
> little
> Wiggle
> pickle
> tickle
> uncle

Where do the two turtles in the story live?

Home

Help your child make up sentences using some of the words in the boxes.

Name _____

Mice can come to this place.
It's such a nice place to race.
They climb in and peek out of the spaces.
Then they stop and wash their faces!

Say the name of each picture. If it has a soft **c** sound, circle the picture. If it has a hard **c** sound, draw a line under it.

RULE

When **c** is followed by **e**, **i**, or **y**, it usually has a soft sound. You can hear the soft **c** sound in **mice**.

1 face

2 cap

3 clock

4 cup

5 pencil

6 cake

7 mice

8 ice

9 celery

Circle the word that will finish each sentence. **Print** it on the line.

1. Cindy and Vince _____ run fast.

can	cage
cape	came

2. They will run in a _____.

mice	race
nice	next

3. The kids _____ to watch.

cap	cane
come	cat

4. Cindy hopes to win first _____.

nice	rice
place	slice

5. The _____ of their shoes are tied.

rice	nice
laces	price

6. They race to the _____.

next	nice
fence	celery

7. It's a tie. They both win _____ prizes.

mice	cereal
nice	price

8. Cindy and Vince have smiling _____.

lace	faces
race	space

9. The kids buy ice-cream _____.

cones	cape
mice	nice

10. Vince _____ wait until the next race.

race	case
can't	nice

 THINK! **Do Cindy and Vince enjoy racing? How do you know?**

Lesson 39
Hard and soft c: Words in context

 Home Help your child group all the hard c words, and then all the soft c words.

Name _____

Gentle giraffes,
Gaze through the trees.
Bigger than giants,
They nibble the leaves.

Say the name of each picture. If the name has a soft **g** sound, circle the picture. If it has a hard **g** sound, draw a line under it.

1. game

2. gym

3. goat

4. page

5. giant

6. gum

7. dragon

8. egg

9. giraffe

The letter **g** can make a hard or a soft sound. Read the words in the box. Listen for the sounds of **g**. Print the words under Soft **g** or Hard **g**.

gift	gem	age	dog	cage	large	good	gum
huge	gave	goat	stage	wag	page	wage	gold
gym	gate	giant	gentle	egg	game	giraffe	give

Soft g Words

_____

_____

_____

_____

_____

_____

_____

_____

_____

Hard g Words

_____

_____

_____

_____

_____

_____

_____

_____

_____

Say a word from the box. Ask your child to spell it and tell if the word has a soft or hard *g* sound.

Name _____

> Read the words in the box. Draw a green line under each word that has a hard **c** or **g** sound. Print each word that has a soft **c** or **g** sound on a line.

giant
price
mice
goat
age
wage
games
huge
cent
ice
gym
cake
race
rice
gas
cone
face

_____   _____

_____   _____

_____   _____

_____   _____

_____   _____

1. nice ___
2. cuff ___
3. ice ___
4. cabin ___
5. lunge ___
6. camel ___
7. game ___
8. race ___
9. gull ___
10. age ___
11. came ___
12. coast ___
13. cake ___
14. coat ___
15. pencil ___
16. gym ___
17. cent ___
18. giant ___
19. gate ___
20. ridge ___
21. care ___
22. goes ___
23. recess ___
24. Vince ___

Draw a red box around each word with a soft g sound. Draw a blue circle around each word with a soft c sound.

25. A giraffe is a gentle giant.

26. You can tell by its kind face.

27. A giraffe is taller than most ceilings.

28. Giraffes think large leaves are delicious.

29. Cereal and vegetables make nice giraffe treats.

30. Zoos with giraffes need tall fences.

31. It costs money to go to the zoo in the city.

32. I need to save fifty cents more to go to the zoo.

Home

Help your child group the words at the top of the page into four lists: hard c, soft c, hard g, and soft g.

Name _____

Phonics & Reading

▶ Read **the story. Print** a word from the story to finish each sentence.

JACK and the MAGIC BEANSTALK

Jack had a magic bean. He planted it in his backyard. The next day he found a huge beanstalk. "Maybe I can climb it," Jack said.

Jack hoped to find a giant at the top with a bag of gold. But Jack got a big surprise! His mother was sitting there at a table.

"You forgot to eat breakfast," she said.

"Sorry, Mom," Jack said.

She gave Jack a plate of pancakes. He drank a cup of milk and ate an apple. Then she sent him home to wash his face.

1. Jack climbed a huge _____.

2. He wanted to find a _____

   and a bag of _____.

3. Jack drank a _____ of milk and

   ate an _____.

4. He went home to wash his _____.

How do you know the bean that Jack had was magical?

Compounds; syllables; le; sounds of c, g: Reading

Phonics & Writing

Jack shared one of his magic beans with you.
Write a story about what grows in your garden.
Use some of the words in the box.

magic	huge	garden	giggle	people
basket	celery	outdoors	corn	maybe

Lesson 42
Compounds; syllables; words with le; sounds of c, g: Writing

Home

Have your child read the story on page 93 and identify the compound and two-syllable words.

Name _____

**Green frogs, tree frogs,
There are so many kinds.
Brown frogs, bullfrogs,
We can't make up our minds.**

> Say the name of each picture. Print its beginning blend on the line. Trace the whole word.

RULE

A **consonant blend** is two or more consonants that come together in a word. Their sounds blend together, but each sound is heard. You can hear **r** blends in **green, tree,** and **frogs.**

1 _____ apes

2 _____ og

3 _____ ee

4 _____ ain

> Use the words above to answer the riddles.

5 I can jump and hop.
You find me in a pond.
I eat bugs.

I am a _____.

6 I am green.
You can find me in a park.
Birds live in me.

I am a _____.

7 I can be small or big.
I make a good toy.
I run on a track.

I am a _____.

8 We grow on vines.
We come in bunches.
We are good to eat.

We are _____.

Lesson 43
Blends with r

Circle the word that names the picture.

1
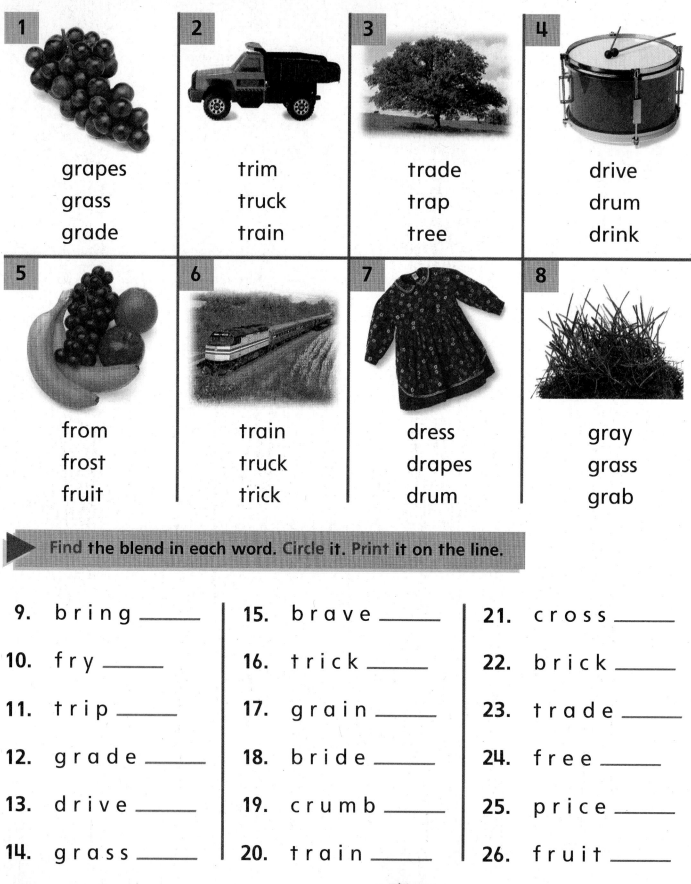

grapes
grass
grade

2

trim
truck
train

3

trade
trap
tree

4

drive
drum
drink

5

from
frost
fruit

6

train
truck
trick

7

dress
drapes
drum

8

gray
grass
grab

Find the blend in each word. Circle it. Print it on the line.

9. b r i n g _____

10. f r y _____

11. t r i p _____

12. g r a d e _____

13. d r i v e _____

14. g r a s s _____

15. b r a v e _____

16. t r i c k _____

17. g r a i n _____

18. b r i d e _____

19. c r u m b _____

20. t r a i n _____

21. c r o s s _____

22. b r i c k _____

23. t r a d e _____

24. f r e e _____

25. p r i c e _____

26. f r u i t _____

Lesson 43
Blends with r

Home

Ask your child to name the pictures
with the same beginning sounds.

The wind blows the clouds.
Sleet turns to snow.
Winter's here again,
And sledding we will go!

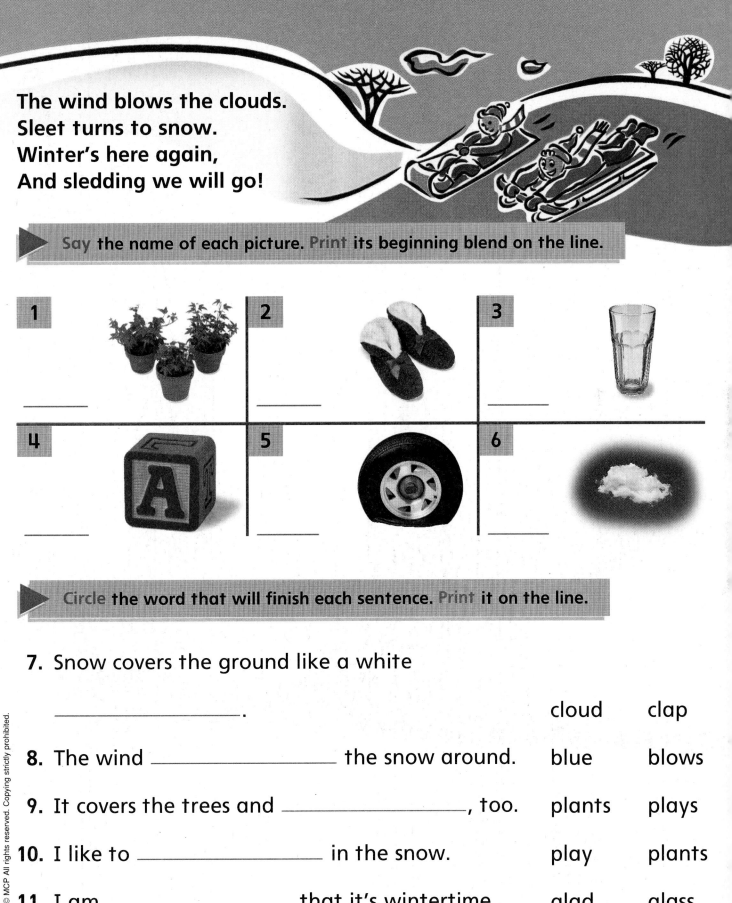

▶ **Say** the name of each picture. **Print** its beginning blend on the line.

1	2	3
_____	_____	_____

4	5	6
_____	_____	_____

▶ **Circle** the word that will finish each sentence. **Print** it on the line.

7. Snow covers the ground like a white

_____.   cloud   clap

8. The wind _____ the snow around.   blue   blows

9. It covers the trees and _____, too.   plants   plays

10. I like to _____ in the snow.   play   plants

11. I am _____ that it's wintertime.   glad   glass

1 Sometimes I ring.
Sometimes I chime.
I tick-tock all the
time.

_____

2 High up on a pole I go.
With the wind I flap
and blow.

_____

3 I hold your food.
Look for me under
your hot dog.

_____

4 I make things
stick for you. I
stick to you, too.

_____

▶ Find a word in the box to finish each sentence.
Print it on the line.

5. I have a new magnifying _____.

6. When I hold it _____ to things, they
   get bigger.

7. A blade of _____ looks like a tree trunk.

8. _____ of wood are really full of holes.

9. A _____ looks like a big black monster!

10. A toy _____ looks like a real plane.

> **Blocks**
> **grass**
> **fly**
> **plane**
> **close**
> **glass**

Ask your child to name other words that
begin with *cl*, *fl*, *pl*, and *bl*.

Name _____

> **Write** the name of each picture. Then **find** the words in the puzzle and **circle** them. **Look** for words that go across and down.

1	2	3	4
5	6	7	8
9	10	11	12

a	x	g	r	a	s	s	t	c	p
m	s	l	i	p	p	e	r	s	l
c	l	o	u	d	n	t	u	g	a
f	f	b	r	e	a	d	c	l	n
r	l	e	b	r	i	c	k	a	t
o	a	x	t	r	e	e	m	s	w
g	g	q	l	p	u	y	y	s	u

1   **2**   **3**   **4**

_____   _____   _____   _____

▶ **Circle** the word that will finish the sentence.
Print it on the line.

5. Every day a _____ comes   from   crow   trim
to my window.

6. It is big and _____.   play   drink   black

7. I am always _____   grade   glad   glass
to see my crow.

8. It likes to get a _____   drum   dress   drink
from our sprinkler.

9. Some days I fix it a _____   plate   play   plum
of crumbs.

10. Crows like to eat bugs

in the _____.   grass   grab   grape

11. They eat bugs in _____, too.   train   trees   truck

Home

Take turns with your child naming
other words with *r* and *l* blends.

Said Squiggle Snake to Slimy Snail,
"Let's slide on the slippery wet grass."
Said Slimy Snail to Squiggle Snake,
"Slow down! You move too fast!"

RULE

Remember that in a **consonant blend** the sounds of the consonants blend together, but each sound is heard. You can hear **s** blends in **slide, snake,** and **squiggle.**

Say the name of each picture. Find its beginning blend in the box. Print it on the line.

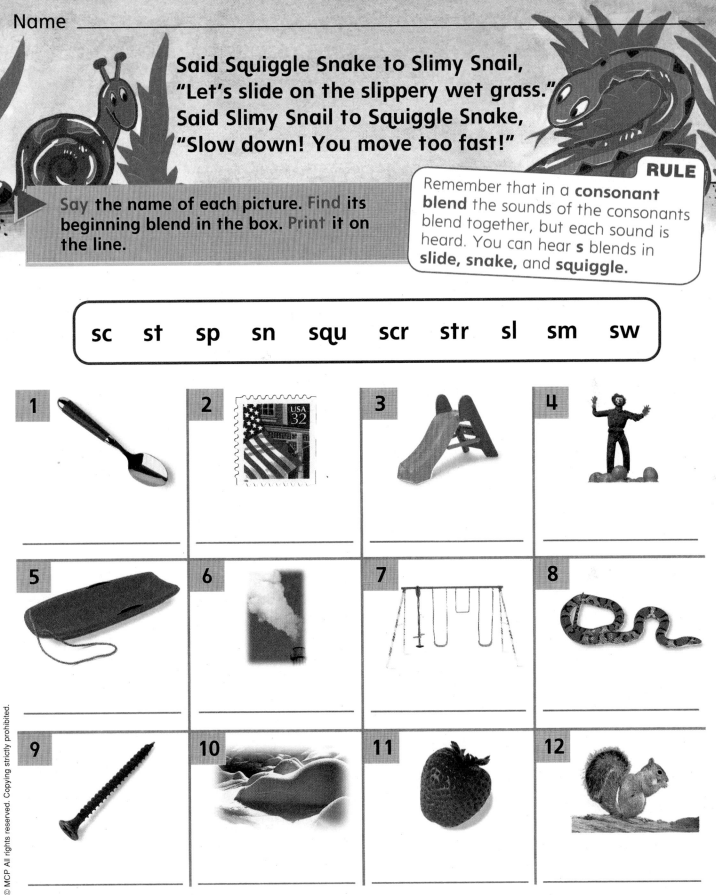

| sc | st | sp | sn | squ | scr | str | sl | sm | sw |

1 _____

2 _____

3 _____

4 _____

5 _____

6 _____

7 _____

8 _____

9 _____

10 _____

11 _____

12 _____

1. Did you ever _____ to think about snakes?

2. Snakes have long, _____ bodies.

3. Snakes can move both fast and _____.

4. _____ have no arms or legs.

5. They still have the _____ to move.

6. Snakes can even _____.

7. Their _____ looks slimy, but it's dry.

8. Snakes _____ some people, but not me.

scare
slim
skin
stop
skill
Snakes
swim
slow

Circle the name of each picture.

9		10		11	
swim	stem	scream	screen	smile	smoke

12		13		14	
stops	steps	snake	sneak	sled	slide

Home

Help your child identify the words in the box that have the same beginning sound.

Name _____

My swing is next to the tree trunk.
My tree fort is near the trunk, too.
Best of all, there's a hole for the chipmunk!
What's left for this tree trunk to do?

RULE

Remember that in a **consonant blend** the sounds of the consonants blend together, but each sound is heard. You can hear blends at the end of **swing** and **trunk**.

▶ Circle **the word that answers each riddle. Print it on the line.**

1 All mail needs these. What are they?

stamps   stumps

_____

2 We can ride on it. What is it?

string   swing

_____

3 An elephant has one. What is it?

skunk   trunk

_____

4 We can eat it. What is it?

toast   list

_____

5 It hides your face. What is it?

task   mask

_____

6 We can sleep in it. What is it?

tent   plant

_____

7 We have two of these. What are they?

lands   hands

_____

8 Fish swim in it. What is it?

tank   wink

_____

9 It can float. What is it?

raft   left

_____

Find the word in the box that names each picture. **Print** it on the line.

milk	skunk	tent	belt	trunk	plants
nest	ring	stamp	raft	desk	mask

1

2

3

_____

4

5

6

_____

7

8

9

_____

10

11

12

_____

Home

Ask your child to name other words that end with *ng*, *sk*, and *mp*.

Name _____

> Read the story. Use a word from the story to finish each sentence. Print the word on the line.

SUNFLOWERS

Wild sunflowers first grew on the plains in the West. Native Americans roasted the seeds and ground them into flour for bread. We still eat sunflower seeds. They are a great food for birds and people.

Spanish explorers brought sunflower plants back to Europe. Now sunflowers grow all over the world. Sunflowers grow in many different sizes. The smallest are only one or two feet tall. The biggest plants are twelve feet tall!

1. Sunflowers first grew on the _____.

2. People ground the seeds into _____.

3. Then they used the flour to make _____.

4. _____ explorers brought sunflowers to Europe.

Why did Spanish explorers bring sunflowers to Europe?

Write a description of a plant or flower, but do not tell its name. Use some of the words in the box. Have your friends guess the name of the plant.

flowers
plants
green
glad
fruit
grow
best
trees
grapes
want

Lesson 48
Review blends: Writing

Home

Ask your child to read his or her description. Guess the name of the plant.

Name _____

Baby bird, baby bird, are you ready?
Baby bird, baby bird, can you try?
Spread your tiny, feathery wings,
For now it is time to fly!

> **RULE**
> Sometimes **y** can stand for the vowel sound of long **e** or long **i**. You can hear the long **e** sound in **baby**.

▶ Circle **each word in which y has a long e sound.**

1. baby	**2.** cry	**3.** happy	**4.** why
5. try	**6.** every	**7.** hurry	**8.** tiny
9. Molly	**10.** sandy	**11.** shy	**12.** puppy
13. penny	**14.** Freddy	**15.** funny	**16.** bunny

▶ Circle **the words in the sentences in which y has a long e sound.**

17. Ty and Molly were helping take care of baby Freddy.

18. They heard Freddy cry in his crib.

19. They went to help in a hurry.

20. They had to try everything to make him happy.

21. Ty read him a funny book about fish that fly.

22. Molly gave him her bunny to play with.

23. Ty made very silly faces.

24. Finally, Freddy was happy.

Circle each word with a y that sounds like long i.

RULE

When **y** is the only vowel at the end of a one-syllable word, **y** usually has the long **i** sound. You can hear the long **i** sound in **try.**

1. try
2. Freddy
3. sly
4. buggy
5. funny

6. bunny
7. dry
8. silly
9. rocky
10. my

11. Ty
12. windy
13. by
14. sky
15. sunny

16. sleepy
17. fly
18. happy
19. muddy
20. cry

21. sneaky
22. lucky
23. shy
24. puppy
25. Molly

26. why
27. jolly
28. baby
29. fry
30. very

Circle each word with y that sounds like long i in the sentences.

31. Why do onions make us cry when we are happy ?

32. Why is the sky blue on a sunny day ?

33. Why do bats fly at night ?

34. Why is a desert dry and a swamp muddy ?

35. Why can a bird fly but not a puppy ?

36. Why do we look silly if we try to fly ?

37. Why is a fox sneaky and sly ?

38. Why is a bunny shy ?

39. Why does a rainy sky make you sleepy ?

40. Do you ever wonder why ?

Home
Ask your child to use three of the circled words on this page in a sentence.

Name _____

▶ **Read** the word in each paw print. If the **y** stands for a long **i** sound, draw a line under the word. If it stands for a long **e** sound, circle the word.

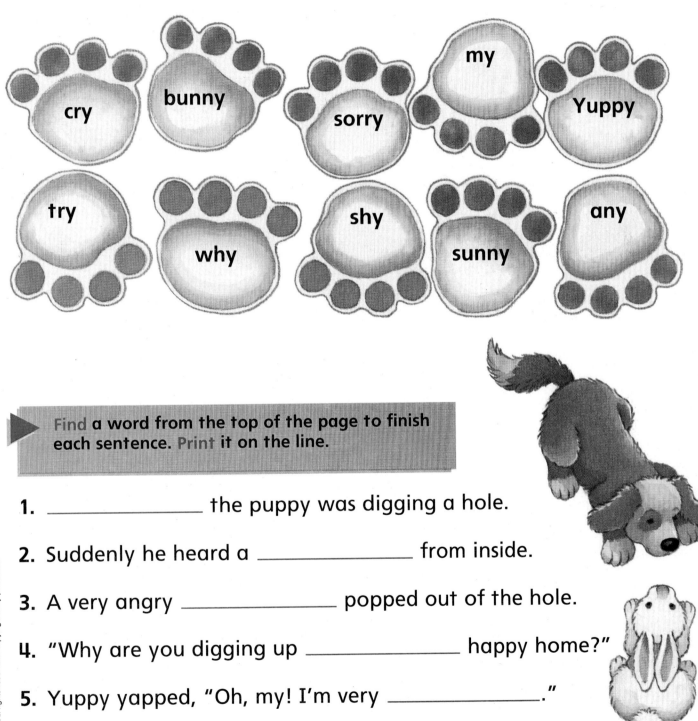

cry

bunny

sorry

my

Yuppy

try

why

shy

sunny

any

▶ **Find** a word from the top of the page to finish each sentence. Print it on the line.

1. _____ the puppy was digging a hole.

2. Suddenly he heard a _____ from inside.

3. A very angry _____ popped out of the hole.

4. "Why are you digging up _____ happy home?"

5. Yuppy yapped, "Oh, my! I'm very _____."

6. "I'll _____ to help you fix it up!"

1
baby
my
fly
fifty
funny

2
sky
sunny
fairy
cry
Bobby

3
dolly
try
sly
kitty
dry

4
lady
penny
shy
fry
happy

5
why
silly
lily
by
bunny

6
my
sixty
fly
Sally
sky

7
jelly
Sandy
my
fry
cry

8
lucky
try
fifty
sky
puppy

9
berry
very
try
sly
any

10
cry
lady
many
sky
by

11
only
city
July
spy
funny

12
my
fly
fifty
happy
silly

Lesson 50
Vowel sounds of y

Help your child find two words that rhyme in each box.

Phonics & Spelling

Say the name of each picture. Find the word inside the grasshopper and spell it. Then print the word on the line.

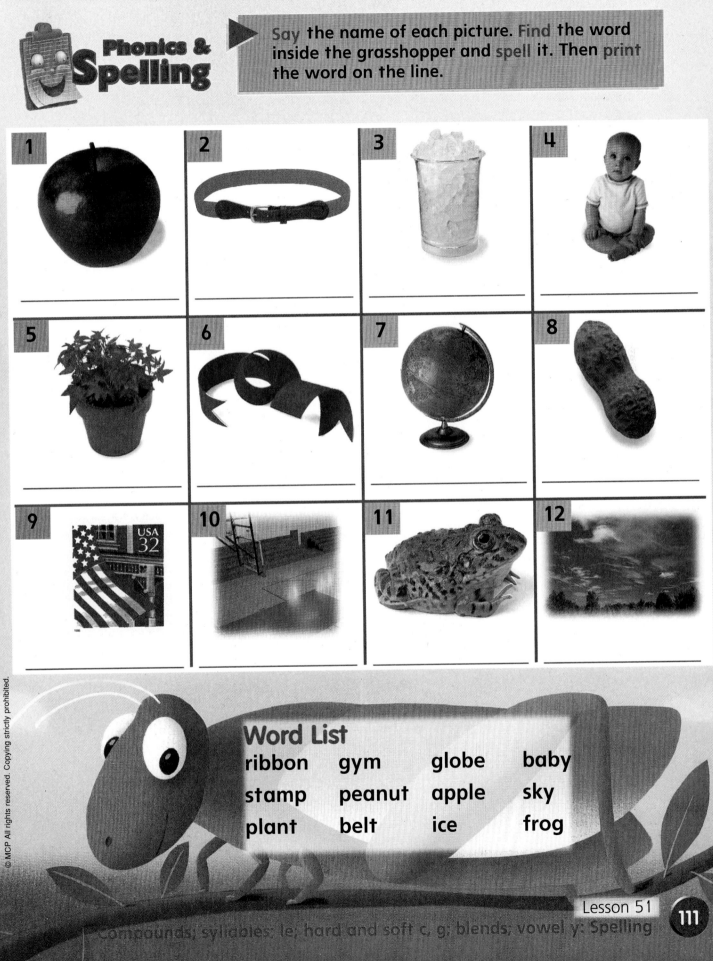

1. _____

2. _____

3. _____

4. _____

5. _____

6. _____

7. _____

8. _____

9. _____

10. _____

11. _____

12. _____

Word List

ribbon	gym	globe	baby
stamp	peanut	apple	sky
plant	belt	ice	frog

Compounds; syllables: le; hard and soft c, g; blends; vowel y: Spelling

Phonics & Writing

Write a story about a grasshopper in a garden. Use some of the words below. Read your story to a friend.

grasshopper	trees	gloves	plants	grow
flowers	smile	glad	fruit	grapes
scarecrow	just	must	best	green

Johnny Appleseed

This book belongs to:

1

Johnny Appleseed wanted people to have juicy fruit to eat. So he cleared the land and planted apple trees.

3

Johnny Appleseed was a friend to Native Americans. No animals ever harmed him.

6

TALK ABOUT IT

Why do you think Johnny Appleseed wanted to plant apple trees?

8

Compounds; syllables; le; hard and soft c, g; blends; vowel y: Take-Home Book

4

Johnny Appleseed walked through Ohio, Indiana, and Illinois. He carried bags of seeds with him. He made many trips.

ILLINOIS

INDIANA

OHIO

2

John Chapman was born in 1774 in Massachusetts. You might know him better as Johnny Appleseed.

For forty years he tramped all over the country. Everywhere he went, he planted apple orchards.

Some people thought Johnny Appleseed was a little odd. He walked barefoot. He often gave away the money that people gave him.

5

7

Compounds; syllables; le; hard and soft c, g; blends; vowel y: Take-Home Book

Name _____

Shiny wet shells on the shore,
More shells down the beach,
There's such a lot to choose from!
Why don't we pick one of each?

▶ Circle the word that will finish each
sentence. Print it on the line.

1. I go to the zoo to see the _____.   chop   chimp   check

2. It smiles to show its _____.   then   teeth   these

3. They are big and _____.   which   what   white

4. It eats bananas by the _____.   bunch   reach   much

5. Once I saw it eat a _____.   that   ship   peach

6. Sometimes it dumps its _____.   wish   dish   swish

7. Then it naps in the _____.   fresh   shut   shade

▶ **Find** two words from the list above that begin with **ch, wh, th,** and
sh. Print them on the lines beside the correct consonant digraph.

8		9	
ch	_____ _____	**th**	_____ _____
10		11	
wh	_____ _____	**sh**	_____ _____

Lesson 53
Consonant digraphs sh, th, wh, ch

1. Chip and I didn't know ——————— to go.

○ where
○ what

2. We decided to go to the mall to ———————.

○ chop
○ shop

3. They sell everything ———————

○ this
○ there

4. There was so ———————to choose from.

○ catch
○ much

5. I couldn't decide ——————— I wanted most.

○ what
○ who

6. Then I saw some model ——————— kits.

○ shirt
○ ship

7. ——————— was what I wanted most.

○ When
○ That

8. I ——————— a clipper ship to make.

○ chose
○ chair

9. ——————— chose a spaceship kit.

○ Choose
○ Chip

10. ——————— we had lunch.

○ Then
○ That

Where do you think Chip bought his model kit?

Lesson 53
Consonant digraphs sh, th, wh, ch

116

Say one of the words in the list. Have your child name the other words that begin with the same sound.

Name _____

> Say the name of each picture. Circle the consonant digraph you hear.

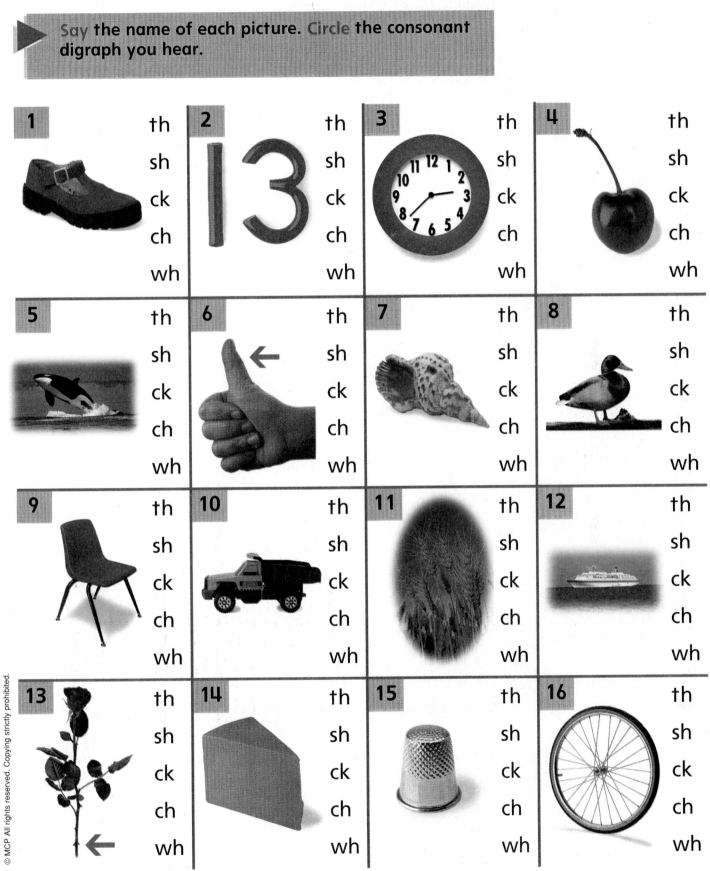

1	th sh ck ch wh	2	th sh ck ch wh	3	th sh ck ch wh	4	th sh ck ch wh
5	th sh ck ch wh	6	th sh ck ch wh	7	th sh ck ch wh	8	th sh ck ch wh
9	th sh ck ch wh	10	th sh ck ch wh	11	th sh ck ch wh	12	th sh ck ch wh
13	th sh ck ch wh	14	th sh ck ch wh	15	th sh ck ch wh	16	th sh ck ch wh

Consonant digraphs sh, th, wh, ch, ck

Read the words in the box and circle the hidden pictures.
Write the words on the lines. Circle the consonant
digraph in each word.

whale	wheel	thumb	clock	truck	duck
fish	peach	chair	thimble	shell	shoe

1. _____   2. _____   3. _____

4. _____   5. _____   6. _____

7. _____   8. _____   9. _____

10. _____   11. _____   12. _____

Lesson 54
Review digraphs sh, th, wh, ch, ck

Home

Have your child find the words with
the same initial digraphs.

Name _____

We work in our garden.
We get down on our knees.
We kneel to plant flowers.
We kneel to pull weeds.

▶ Read each sentence. Find the picture it tells about. Write the sentence letter under the picture.

1

a. John has a knot in the rope.
b. I know what is in the box.
c. Joan turned the knob.

_____   _____

2

a. Theo will knock down the pile.
b. Mom cut it with a knife.
c. She knocks on the door.

_____   _____

3

a. The knight wore armor.
b. Tad's knee needs a patch.
c. Grandma likes to knit.

_____   _____

▶ Find a word in the box that answers each riddle. Print it on the line.

4. Something that can cut _____

5. Someone who wore armor _____

6. Something you can tie _____

knife
knot
knight

1. I _____ how to do many things.   know   knot

2. I can spread butter with a _____.   knot   knife

3. I can touch my _____ to my chin.   knees   knew

4. I can tie _____.   knots   knits

5. I can turn the _____ of a door.   knee   knob

6. I can read about _____.   know   knights

7. I can _____ a sweater.   knit   knife

8. I've _____ how to do these
   things for a long time.   knit   known

Think of a word that begins with **kn** and rhymes with
each word. Print the word on the line.

9.   snow   10.   block   11.   wife

_____   _____   _____

12.   blew   13.   see   14.   hot

_____   _____   _____

15.   own   16.   sit   17.   sob

_____   _____   _____

Ask your child to make up sentences
using the *kn* words on the page.

Name _____

The small earthworm wriggles
And wrenches to stay.
The hungry wren wrestles,
But the worm gets away!

Find the word in the box that will finish each sentence. Print it on the line.

RULE

You can hear the consonant digraph **wr** in **wriggles** and **wren**.

wren	wreck	wrap	wrestle	write
wrist	wrench	wrecker	wrong	wriggle

1. To move around is to _____.

2. The opposite of **right** is _____.

3. A small bird is a _____.

4. A thing that is ruined is a _____.

5. To hide a gift in paper is to _____ it.

6. When you put a story on paper, you _____.

7. Your _____ holds your hand to your arm.

8. A truck that clears away wrecks is a _____.

9. A kind of tool is a _____.

10. One way to fight is to _____.

**Find a word in the box that answers each riddle.
Print it on the line.**

wren	wrecker	wriggle	wrong	wrist
wrench	wreath	writer	typewriter	wrinkle

1
I am a useful tool.
I can fix things.
What am I?

_____

2
I am the opposite of **right**.
I rhyme with **song**.
What am I?

_____

3
I can fly.
I like to sing.
What am I?

_____

4
I am round and pretty.
You can hang me up.
What am I?

_____

5
I am next to a hand.
I can twist and bend.
What am I?

_____

6
I make letters.
People press my keys.
What am I?

_____

7
I am a big truck.
I tow things away.
What am I?

_____

8
I write stories. They can be
real or make-believe.
What am I?

_____

9
I am a fold in a dress.
I am a crease in a face.
What am I?

_____

10
I am another word for **squirm**.
I rhyme with **giggle**.
What am I?

_____

Lesson 56
Consonant digraph wr

Home

Ask your child to circle the letters *wr*
in each word and say the word.

Name _____

Phonics & Reading

▶ Read the story. Use a word from the story to finish each sentence. Print the word on the line.

Chipmunks

The chipmunk's brown coat with its black-and-white stripes helps it blend in with the rocks and bushes. A chipmunk can sit very still. Then it wriggles its nose and twitches its whiskers.

A chipmunk is a shy animal. A sound it does not know may chase it back into its hole. A chipmunk can move fast.

Chipmunks carry food in their cheek pouches. They store nuts and grain in their dens. Then they know they will not go hungry when winter comes.

1. This story is about _____.

2. A chipmunk is a _____ animal.

3. Its brown coat has black-and- _____ stripes.

4. The chipmunk _____ its nose.

THINK! What might scare a chipmunk?

Imagine you are a wildlife watcher. Choose one of the animals pictured below. Write what you know about it. Some of the words below may help you.

| when | shell | wriggle | whiskers | flock |
| know | their | show | bunch | chirp |

Lesson 57
Review digraphs: Writing

Home

Say a word from the list and have your child name another word with the same initial or final sound.

Name _____

So many strawberries to pick,
It's hard to know where to start!
Let's pick the largest ones
And bake them in a tart.

RULE

An **r** after a vowel makes the vowel sound different from the usual short or long sound. You can hear the **ar** sound in **hard, start,** and **largest.**

▶ Find **the word in the box that will finish each sentence.** Print **it on the line.**

apart	star	hard	part	car
hardly	start	large	jars	

1. I picked out a new model _____ kit.

2. I got two _____ of paint, too.

3. I could hardly wait to _____ on it.

4. I glued it so the car wouldn't fall _____.

5. There were small parts and _____ parts.

6. The tires were _____ to fit, but I did it.

7. I stuck gold _____ stickers on the sides.

8. I could _____ believe it when it was done.

9. The best _____ was showing it to my friends.

Finish each sentence. Use a word that rhymes with the word beside the sentence. Print it on the line.

1. A shark is a very _____ animal.

2. It lives in the deep, _____ part of the ocean.

3. It can grow to be very _____.

4. A shark's teeth are very _____.

5. It has no problem tearing food _____.

6. I live _____ from the ocean.

7. I like to visit the animal _____.

8. It's not far from my house by _____.

9. I can watch the sharks there free from _____.

| part |
| bark |
| barge |
| carp |
| start |
| star |
| lark |
| tar |
| farm |

Print three rhyming words under each word.

| 10 | mark | 11 | start | 12 | hard |

Home

Ask your child to circle all the words with *ar* in the sentences on page 125.

Name _____

You love corn a lot.
But I love it more.
We buy popcorn at the movies
And sweet corn at the store.

Food List

> Read each riddle. Answer it with a word that rhymes with the word beside the riddle. Print it on the line.

RULE

An **r** after a vowel makes the vowel sound different from the usual short or long sound. You can hear the **or** sound in **corn** and **more**.

1. Something we can pop and eat _____ | horn |

2. Something on a unicorn _____ | born |

3. Something we eat with _____ | cork |

4. Something with rain, wind, and thunder _____ | form |

5. Something we can play or watch _____ | port |

6. Something sharp on a rose _____ | born |

7. Something beside the sea _____ | tore |

8. Something to close up a bottle _____ | pork |

9. Something that gives us light _____ | porch |

Help the horse get to the barn. **Find** the words in the maze with **ar** and **or**. **Follow** them to get to the barn. **Write** each word on the line beside the puzzle.

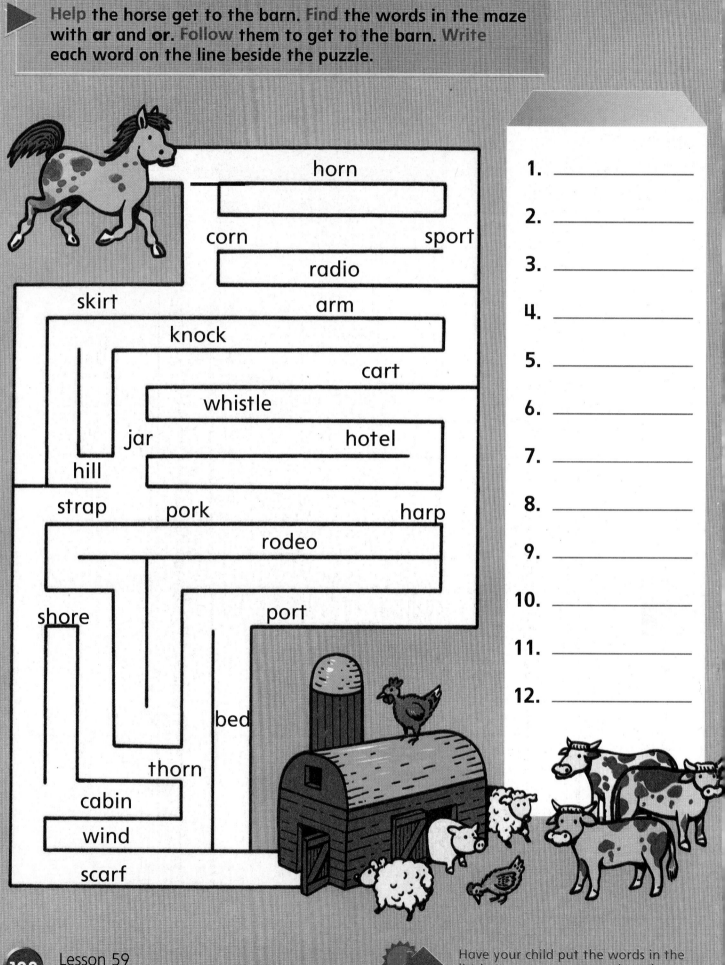

horn

corn
sport

radio

skirt
arm

knock

cart

whistle

jar
hotel

hill

strap
pork
harp

rodeo

shore
port

bed

thorn

cabin

wind

scarf

1. _____
2. _____
3. _____
4. _____
5. _____
6. _____
7. _____
8. _____
9. _____
10. _____
11. _____
12. _____

Lesson 59
Review words with ar, or

Home

Have your child put the words in the list in two groups: *ar* words and *or* words.

Name _____

See that bird in the old fir tree?
She'll turn around and chirp at me.
She chirps and chirps her song all day
I hope she never ever goes away.

RULE

An **r** after a vowel makes the vowel sound different from the usual short or long sound. You can hear the **ir** sound in **bird,** the **ur** sound in **turn,** and the **er** sound in **her.**

▶ Circle each word that has the same vowel sound as the name of the picture.

1 ir
first
fork
skirt
shirt
girl
bird

2 ur
curb
purse
card
nurse
fur
turtle

3 er
batter
letter
hammer
park
clerk
fern

▶ Find the name of each picture in the words above. Print the name on the line.

4 _____

5 _____

6 _____

7 _____

8 _____

9 _____

10 _____

11 _____

Lesson 60
Words with ir, er, ur

 129

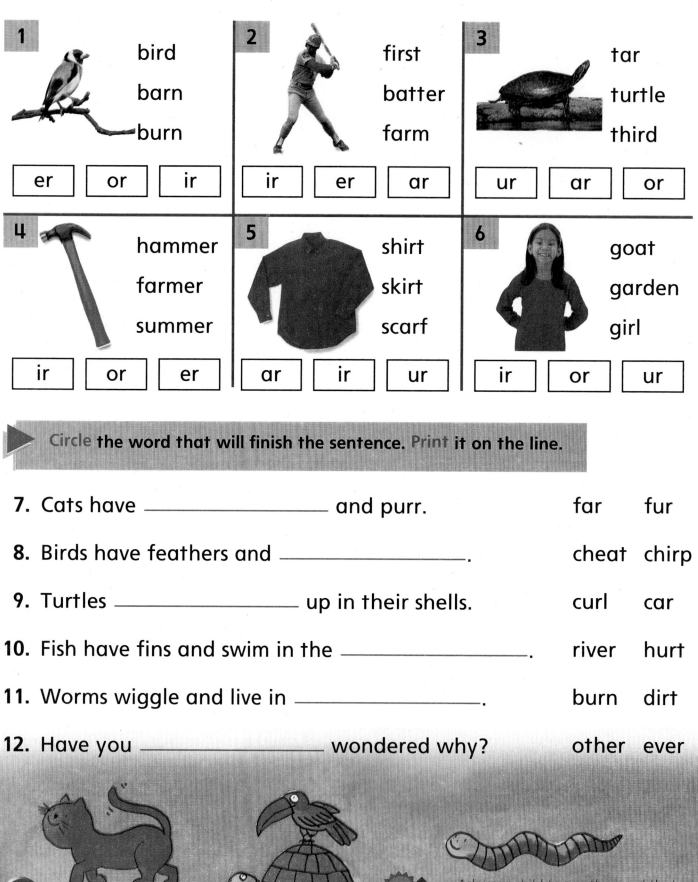

1

bird
barn
burn

| er | or | ir |

2

first
batter
farm

| ir | er | ar |

3

tar
turtle
third

| ur | ar | or |

4

hammer
farmer
summer

| ir | or | er |

5

shirt
skirt
scarf

| ar | ir | ur |

6

goat
garden
girl

| ir | or | ur |

Circle the word that will finish the sentence. Print it on the line.

7. Cats have _____ and purr.   far   fur

8. Birds have feathers and _____.   cheat   chirp

9. Turtles _____ up in their shells.   curl   car

10. Fish have fins and swim in the _____.   river   hurt

11. Worms wiggle and live in _____.   burn   dirt

12. Have you _____ wondered why?   other   ever

Home   Ask your child to say the word that names the picture and identify the vowel sound with r.

Name _____

> **Find** the word in the box that will finish the sentence.
> **Print** it on the line.

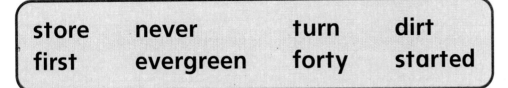

store	never	turn	dirt
first	evergreen	forty	started

1. This is the _____ tree I ever planted.

2. It is a fir tree called an _____.

3. That means it will _____ change colors.

4. We bought it at a plant _____.

5. We _____ by digging a deep hole.

6. Afterwards we put the _____ back in the hole.

7. It is my _____ to water the tree today.

8. In _____ years, this tree will be huge.

> **Write** each word from the box on the tree that shows its vowel sound.

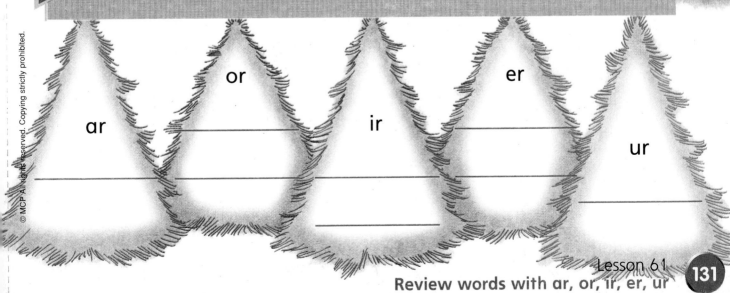

ar

or _____

ir _____

er

ur _____

Find the vowel followed by r in each word. Print the two letters on the line. Then print the number of the picture with the same two letters.

1. part   ar   1

2. verse _____ __

3. turn _____ __

4. pork _____ __

5. first _____ __

6. party _____ __

7. third _____ __

8. bark _____ __

9. fern _____ __

10. storm _____ __

11. her _____ __

12. chirp _____ __

13. park _____ __

14. horse _____ __

15. fur _____ __

16. skirt _____ __

17. curb _____ __

18. short _____ __

19. purse _____ __

20. under _____ __

21. hard _____ __

22. burn _____ __

1. car   2. horn   3. bird   4. hammer   5. turtle

132   Lesson 61
Review words with ar, or, ir, er, ur

Say a word on this page and ask your child to name other words that have the same vowel followed by r.

Name _____

Phonics & Spelling

▶ Say and spell each word below. Then print the word in the basket where it belongs.

Word List

shoe	beach	truck	wheel	car	girl
write	thorn	why	chair	wrong	nurse
knock	fork	knob	wish	bath	block

sh
1. _____
2. _____

th
3. _____
4. _____

wh
5. _____
6. _____

ch
7. _____
8. _____

ck
9. _____
10. _____

kn
11. _____
12. _____

ir, ur
13. _____
14. _____

wr
15. _____
16. _____

ar, or
17. _____
18. _____

Phonics & Writing

> **Pretend** that someone you know just won a prize for growing the biggest pumpkin in town. **Write** a story about it for the newspaper. **Use** some of the words in the box.

dirt	water	when	each	know
this	brother	write	where	little
show	start	rocks	large	yard

_____

_____

_____

_____

_____

_____

Book Corner

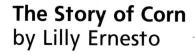

The Story of Corn
by Lilly Ernesto

Learn how corn is grown and about the different kinds of corn in this story with pictures.

134 Lesson 62
Words with sh, th, wh, ch, ck, kn, wr;
r-controlled vowels: Writing

Home Ask your child to spell one word from each basket on page 133.

Is it important to save the forests?

TALK ABOUT IT

Bert was
shocked.
"That tree
told me to
go home."
"What sort
of trees
talk?" the
boss asked.

6

FOLD

FOLD

This book belongs to

_____

THE TALKING FOREST

Bert started with
a big, old tree.
He laid his chain
saw against the
hard bark. A furry
squirrel scolded Bert.

3

1

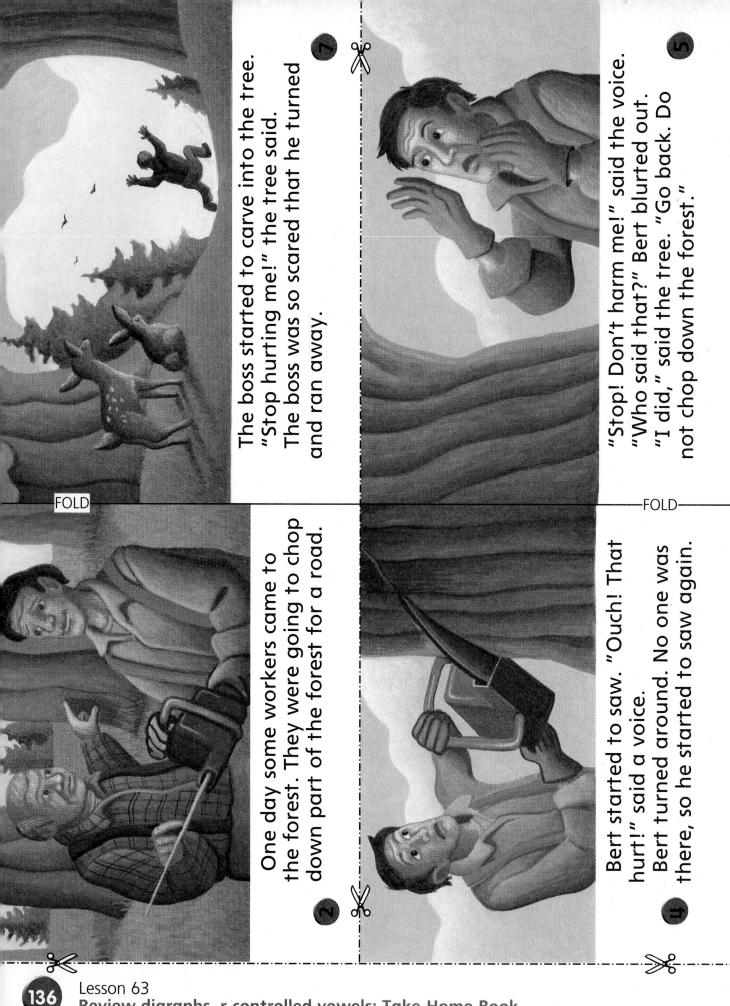

7

The boss started to carve into the tree. "Stop hurting me!" the tree said. The boss was so scared that he turned and ran away.

5

"Stop! Don't harm me!" said the voice. "Who said that?" Bert blurted out. "I did," said the tree. "Go back. Do not chop down the forest."

FOLD

FOLD

2

One day some workers came to the forest. They were going to chop down part of the forest for a road.

4

Bert started to saw. "Ouch! That hurt!" said a voice. Bert turned around. No one was there, so he started to saw again.

UNIT 4 CHECKUP

Name _____

Fill in the bubble beside the name of each picture.

1
- ○ nice
- ○ mice
- ○ rice

2
- ○ giraffe
- ○ goat
- ○ giant

3
- ○ turn
- ○ train
- ○ turkey

4
- ○ popcorn
- ○ cupcake
- ○ pencil

5
- ○ beach
- ○ dirt
- ○ bird

6
- ○ clock
- ○ cherry
- ○ check

7
- ○ block
- ○ black
- ○ blot

8
- ○ sneak
- ○ snake
- ○ snore

9
- ○ skunk
- ○ skate
- ○ skill

10
- ○ bun
- ○ bunny
- ○ baby

11
- ○ try
- ○ cry
- ○ shy

12
- ○ ship
- ○ shop
- ○ shell

13
- ○ trunk
- ○ think
- ○ thirteen

14
- ○ chair
- ○ table
- ○ turtle

15
- ○ wrap
- ○ write
- ○ wriggle

Lesson 64

Compounds; le; hard and soft c, g; blends; vowel y; digraphs; r-controlled vowels: Checkup

137

UNIT 4 CHECKUP

knife	snake	garden	Maybe
farm	basket	pepper	who
corn	broccoli	fresh	glad

1. Many kinds of vegetables grow on a _____.

2. First, let's look in the _____.

3. The _____ is green and bushy.

4. We need a _____ to cut the stalks.

5. We can put this green _____ in a salad.

6. _____ I can eat one of the carrots now.

7. Oh! A green _____ just slid under a rock.

8. Let's go pick some sweet yellow _____!

9. We can put it in this straw _____.

10. Vegetables taste best when they are _____.

11. I'm _____ it's almost time to eat.

12. Now _____ will cook them for us?

Ask your child to make up new sentences containing some of the words from the box.

Home

Read Aloud

COUNTDOWN

9

The spaceship is ready.

8

The countdown is steady.

7

The green lights all glow.

6

All systems are go.

5

The crew is all set.

4

So start up the jets.

3

Big engines roar!

2

Only two seconds more.

1

We're set to lift off.

0

What do you say when a spaceship takes off?

THINK!

Do you think taking off in a spaceship would be exciting? Why or why not?

Home Letter

Dear Family,

Your child will be blasting off and exploring space as our class studies contractions, word endings, and suffixes.

At-Home Activities

Here are some activities you and your child might like to do together.

▶ Ask your child to draw a picture of outer space. Then make a list together of the things included. Point out any plurals in the list such as planets, stars, comets, and moons.

▶ With your child look through newspapers and magazines for articles about space. Read the articles and circle words with contractions (we've, can't) and suffixes (dark**ness**, slow**ly**).

Book Corner

You and your child might enjoy reading these books together. Look for them in your local library.

The Moon and You
by E.C. Krupp

This book provides young readers with a light-hearted introduction to the moon.

Moongame
by Frank Asch

In this enchanting story, Bear learns to play hide-and-seek with the moon—and with surprising results!

Sincerely,

Name _____

I'll build a rocket.
We'll go to the moon.
We'll explore outer space.
But, you'll be home by noon.

▶ **Print** a word from the box that means the same as the two words beside each line.

you'll	they'll	she'll
we'll	I'll	he'll

1. I will _____

2. he will _____

3. we will _____

4. they will _____

5. she will _____

6. you will _____

▶ **Print** the short form of the two underlined words in each sentence.

7. I will get in the boat after you. _____

8. He will climb aboard next. _____

9. She will join us, too. _____

10. They will hop in for the ride. _____

11. All aboard? Oh, no! We will sink! _____

Print a word from the box that means the same as the two words beside each line.

RULE
Some contractions are formed with the word **not**.
does not = doesn't

can't	couldn't	weren't	doesn't	don't
didn't	aren't	isn't	won't	haven't

1. are not _____

2. do not _____

3. did not _____

4. will not _____

5. were not _____

6. is not _____

7. could not _____

8. can not _____

9. does not _____

10. have not _____

Print two words that mean the same as each underlined word.

11. Mitten the kitten <u>can't</u> get down from the tree.

_____

12. She <u>isn't</u> brave enough to climb down.

_____

13. She <u>doesn't</u> know what to do.

_____

14. We <u>didn't</u> have any problem getting her down.

_____

15. "<u>Aren't</u> you a lucky kitten to have friends to help?"

_____

With your child, take turns making up contractions with the words *will* and *not*.

Name _____

Circle two words in each sentence that can be made into one of the contractions in the box. Print the contraction on the line.

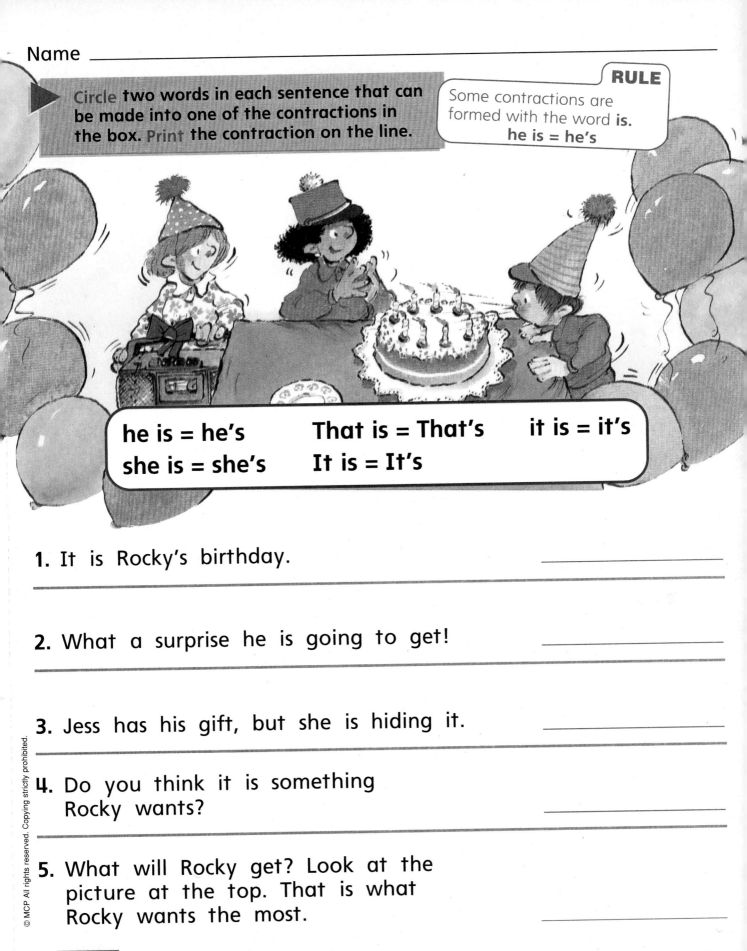

| he is = he's | That is = That's | it is = it's |
| she is = she's | It is = It's | |

1. It is Rocky's birthday. _____

_____

2. What a surprise he is going to get! _____

_____

3. Jess has his gift, but she is hiding it. _____

4. Do you think it is something
Rocky wants? _____

5. What will Rocky get? Look at the
picture at the top. That is what
Rocky wants the most. _____

THINK! **Why does Jess hide
Rocky's present?**

Lesson 66
Contractions with is

RULE

Some contractions are formed with the word **have.**
 You have = You've
 I have = I've
 We have = We've
 They have = They've

▶ **Print** the contraction that means the same as the underlined words in each sentence.

1

I have made you smile.

_____ made you smile.

2

We have shown you tricks.

_____ shown you tricks.

3

They have tossed a ball with their noses.

_____ tossed a ball with their noses.

4

You have had a good time.

_____ had a good time.

THINK! **Where did these things happen?**

Lesson 66
Contractions with have

144

Write contractions and have your child write the two words that make each one.

Name _____

▶ **Print two words that mean the same as the underlined word in each sentence.**

1. <u>Let's</u> have a party. _____

2. <u>We'll</u> ask our friends to come. _____

3. <u>I'm</u> going to pop popcorn. _____

4. <u>He's</u> going to bring some lemonade. _____

5. <u>She's</u> going to bring some cupcakes. _____

6. <u>They're</u> going to bring games. _____

7. <u>We're</u> going to have fun! _____

▶ **Print the contraction that means the same as the two words beside the line.**

8. you are _____

9. I am _____

10. let us _____

11. we are _____

12. he is _____

13. I will _____

14. she is _____

15. it is _____

16. they are _____

17. we will _____

18. they will _____

19. he will _____

Print the letter of each contraction next to the words that have the same meaning.

a. we're	**b.** you'll	**c.** it's	**d.** can't	**e.** I'm
f. he's	**g.** won't	**h.** let's	**i.** don't	**j.** she's
k. you're	**l.** isn't	**m.** he'll	**n.** we'll	**o.** I'll
p. I've	**q.** they'll	**r.** she'll	**s.** we've	**t.** aren't

1. we will _____   **2.** we are _____   **3.** will not _____   **4.** he is _____

5. you will _____   **6.** let us _____   **7.** can not _____   **8.** it is _____

9. is not _____   **10.** you are _____   **11.** they will _____   **12.** I am _____

13. do not _____   **14.** I have _____   **15.** she will _____   **16.** she is _____

17. he will _____   **18.** we have _____   **19.** are not _____   **20.** I will _____

Find a word in the box that will finish each sentence. **Print** it on the line.

Let's
I'm
It's
I'll
don't
we're

21. _____ go skating in the park.

22. _____ time for us to go.

23. I _____ want to be late.

24. I know _____ ready now, are you?

25. _____ help you find your skates.

26. I think _____ going to have fun.

Lesson 67
Review contractions

Home

With your child, take turns making up a sentence for each contraction.

146

Name _____

Phonics & Reading

▶ Read the letter. Print a contraction on the line to finish each sentence.

Dear Mom and Dad,

   I can't believe I've been at Space Camp for four days. I'm having so much fun I don't ever want to leave!

   We're being trained like real astronauts. We're learning about rockets and space travel. Yesterday we made models of rockets and launched them. It's hard work. There's so much to remember.

   Today I'm going in the Moonwalk Trainer. It's a special chair that lets you feel what it's like to walk on the moon. I can't wait.

                              Love,
                              Cara

1. Cara said, "I _____ believe _____ been at Space Camp for four days."

2. "_____ being trained like real astronauts," she said.

3. "_____ hard work. _____ so much to remember."

 **What would you like to learn at Space Camp?**

Pretend **you want to go** to Space Camp.
Fill out the following form to apply.
Use some of the words in the box.

it's	space	you've
shuttle	can't	they're
you're	rockets	isn't
I'm	learn	know
I'll	work	fly

Space Camp Application

Name _____

How did you hear about Space Camp?

_____

_____

What do you think you'll do at Space Camp?

_____

_____

Why do you want to go to Space Camp?

_____

_____

Home

Ask your child to tell what words make
the contractions in the list above.

Name _____

Games, books, brushes,
Sandwiches and candy bars.
What other things shall I pack
For a spaceship trip to Mars?

▶ Circle the word that will finish each
sentence. Print it on the line.

RULE

When **s** or **es** is added to a word it forms the plural. Plural means "more than one." If a word ends in **x, z, ss, sh,** or **ch,** usually add **es** to make it mean more than one. For other words just add **s.**

one brush   two **brushes**
one sandwich   many **sandwiches**
one book   three **books**

---

1 At the zoo we saw some

seal   seals

_____.

2 We like to eat fresh

peach peaches

_____.

3 We have toys in three

box   boxes

_____.

4 June will use a

brush   brushes

_____.

5 Ed's mom gave him a

cap   caps

_____.

6 Just look at those

dog   dogs

_____.

7 Look at those shiny

star   stars

_____.

8 The box was used for

mitten   mittens

_____.

Read each shopping list. **Finish** each word by adding the ending **s** or **es**. **Print** the ending on the line.

1

Steve's List

1. 2 book _____ to read

2. 3 paintbrush _____

3. 6 red pencil _____

4. 2 jar _____ of paste

2

Peggy's List

1. 5 block _____

2. 2 box _____ of clay

3. 3 top _____ to spin

4. 2 puzzle _____

3

Pam's List

1. 8 dish _____

2. 8 cup _____

3. 4 glass _____

4. 2 patch _____ for jeans

4

Ron's List

1. 7 apple _____

2. 5 peach _____

3. 4 sandwich _____

4. 2 bunch _____ of grapes

Home

Ask your child to make up a list of objects using endings -s, -es.

Name _____

Floating and bobbing,
We drifted in space.
We tried hard to run,
But just stayed in one place.

Add **ing** to each base word. Print the new word on the line.

1. sleep _____

2. jump _____

3. play _____

4. help _____

5. start _____

6. work _____

7. fish _____

8. turn _____

Add **ing** to the word beside each sentence. Print the new word on the line.

9. We are _____ for the bus.

10. Doris and Mark are _____ rope.

11. Sam is _____ for the bus.

12. Bart's dog is _____ with him.

13. Terry is _____ his lunch.

14. Meg is _____ a book.

15. Now the bus is _____ our corner!

| wait |
| jump |
| look |
| stay |
| hold |
| read |
| turn |

Add ed to each base word. Print the new word on the line. Use the new words to finish the sentences.

1 look _____

2 want _____

3 help _____

4 leap _____

5 fix _____

6 paint _____

7. Jess _____ me catch a frog.

8. We _____ a frog for a pet.

9. We _____ everywhere for frogs.

10. Suddenly a frog _____ over a rock.

11. We _____ up a box for a frog home.

Print each base word on the line.

12 locked _____

13 marched _____

14 dreamed _____

15 played _____

16 cleaned _____

17 passed _____

18 watched _____

19 wanted _____

20 missed _____

Lesson 70
Inflectional ending -ed

 Home

With your child, take turns acting out each base word; then add ed.

Name _____

Add **es** or **ed** to the base word in the cap to finish each sentence. Print the new word on the line.

1. The girls _____ baseball after school.

2. Randy always watches and _____ for Jean's team to win.

3. The ball comes fast and _____ past Jean's bat. Strike one!

4. The pitcher throws and the ball

   _____ toward the plate.

5. Jean swings as the ball _____ by.

6. This time Jean has not _____.

7. Randy _____ up out of his seat.

8. He _____ until he was hoarse.

play

wish

brush

buzz

pass

miss

jump

cheer

Add **s** or **es** to each base word in the box. Print the new word on the line.

| see | fox | bush | patch | mail | line |

9. _____   10. _____   11. _____

12. _____   13. _____   14. _____

1. Dad goes _____ in the stream.

fishing
fished

2. While the time _____, he looks around.

passes
passing

3. Yesterday some quacking ducks

_____ by.

floats
floated

4. Three baby ducks _____ their mother.

followed
following

5. Frogs were _____ in and out of the water.

jumping
jumps

6. They were _____ for bugs to eat.

looking
looked

7. Some birds were _____ each other.

helped
helping

8. While one _____ the nest, the other looked for food.

watched
watching

9. They _____ to feed their hungry babies.

needs
needed

10. Dad _____ looking around as much as he likes fishing.

liking
likes

THINK

What did Dad see while he was fishing?

Lesson 71
Review endings -s, -es, -ed, -ing

Home Take turns identifying the base word and the ending for each circled word.

Name _____

Add **ing** to the base word in the box.
Print **the new word on the line.**

RULE
When a short vowel word ends in a single consonant, usually double the consonant before adding **ing**.
stop + ing = stopping

	plan

1. Maria and Jess were _____ to go shopping.

	jog

2. First they went _____ in the park.

	swing

3. Children were _____ on the swings.

4. Some horseback riders were

_____ around.

	trot
	walk

5. Other people were _____ along a path.

	hop

6. They saw two bunnies _____ by.

	snap

7. A turtle was _____ at a bug.

	roast

8. A man was _____ hot dogs.

	beg

9. His dog was _____ for one.

	Run

10. "_____ in the park was fun," said Maria.

11. "Now let's go _____,"
Jess said.

	shop

What time of year is this?

To make a word tell about the past, usually add **ed**. If a short vowel word ends in a single consonant, usually double the consonant before adding **ed**.
I **skip** on my way home.
Yesterday I **skipped,** too.

▶ Add **ed** to the word beside each sentence to make it tell about the past. Print the word on the line.

1. My dog _____ his tail when I got home.

2. He _____ up on me with a happy smile.

3. When I _____ him, my hand got muddy.

4. "Wags, you need to be _____!"

5. I _____ him up.

6. Then I _____ him in the tub.

7. He _____ around in the water.

8. He _____ water everywhere!

9. I laughed as I _____ him.

10. When Wags _____, he was clean but I was a mess!

11. I _____ up the mess.

12. Then I _____ with Wags.

wag

hop

pat

scrub

pick

dip

jump

splash

watch

stop

clean

play

THINK! How do you think Wags got muddy?

Lesson 72
Inflectional ending -ed

Take turns with your child saying a word and spelling it with the -ed ending.

Name _____

▶ Circle the word that finishes each sentence. Print it on the line.

RULE
If a word ends with a silent **e**, drop the **e** before adding **ing** or **ed**.
I **bake** cookies with my mom.
We **baked** cookies yesterday.
We are **baking** cookies today, too.

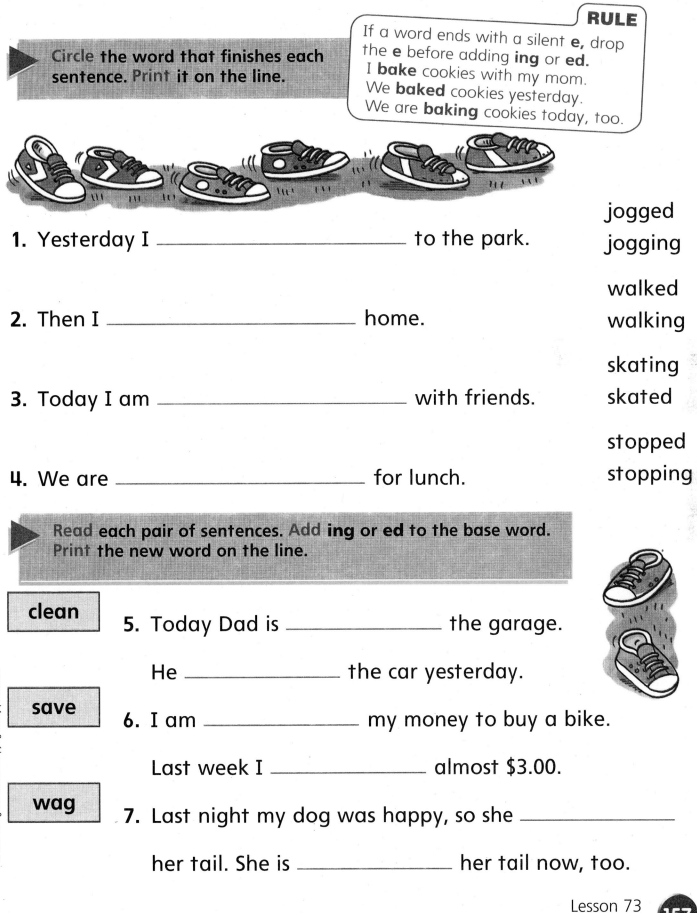

1. Yesterday I _____ to the park.

jogged
jogging

2. Then I _____ home.

walked
walking

3. Today I am _____ with friends.

skating
skated

4. We are _____ for lunch.

stopped
stopping

▶ Read each pair of sentences. Add **ing** or **ed** to the base word. Print the new word on the line.

clean

5. Today Dad is _____ the garage.

He _____ the car yesterday.

save

6. I am _____ my money to buy a bike.

Last week I _____ almost $3.00.

wag

7. Last night my dog was happy, so she _____

her tail. She is _____ her tail now, too.

▶ **Add ing to each base word. Print the new word on the line.**

1. ride _____

2. fry _____

3. rub _____

4. hide _____

5. frame _____

6. dig _____

7. take _____

8. jump _____

9. poke _____

10. ship _____

11. pack _____

12. quit _____

▶ **Add ed to each base word. Print the new word on the line.**

13. pin _____

14. rock _____

15. chase _____

16. hop _____

17. march _____

18. bake _____

19. wish _____

20. drop _____

21. hope _____

22. quack _____

158 Lesson 73
Inflectional endings -ing, -ed

With your child take turns choosing a word, adding an ending, and using it in a sentence.

Name _____

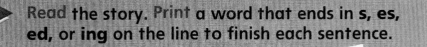

Read the story. Print a word that ends in **s, es, ed,** or **ing** on the line to finish each sentence.

Seeing Stars

Have you ever looked up in the sky and wondered about the stars? Some stars are huge masses of fire like the sun. Many of these stars may have worlds traveling around them just as the Earth we live on travels around our sun. Astronomers have discovered planets around some stars.

We are not traveling alone. Some of the stars you see are not stars at all. They are other planets going around our sun. Nine planets have been discovered so far. Other planets may be waiting far out in space for someone to find them.

1. Have you ever wondered about the _____?

2. Some stars are huge _____ of fire.

3. Nine planets have been _____ around our sun.

4. Other planets may be _____ to be found.

THINK!

Do you think other planets will be discovered? Why or why not?

Lesson 74

Review -s, -es, -ed, -ing: Reading

Phonics & Writing

Imagine you are an astronaut on a spacecraft traveling to other planets. Part of your job is to write in your log book what happens every day. Write about what you saw today. Use some of the words in the box.

wanted	likes	wishes	passes	watched
stars	colors	planets	seeing	traveled
rings	moons	waiting	space	floating

Date _____

_____

_____

_____

_____

_____

_____

_____

_____

Home

Ask your child to find words with -s, -es, -ed, -ing in the story on page 159.

Name _____

Moon rocks are colorful,
Moon dust is wonderful.
But I must be truthful,
They aren't very useful!

▶ **Add** the ending **ful** to each base word.
Print the new word on the line. **Use** the
new words to finish the sentences.

RULE
You can make a new word by
adding the ending **ful** to a base
word.
color + ful = colorful

1. care _____

2. cheer _____

3. wonder _____

4. use _____

5. Pablo thought a skateboard would be very _____.

6. He promised to be _____ if he got one.

7. His family looked _____ when they gave
him his gift.

8. It was a skateboard! What a _____ gift!

▶ **Draw** a box around each base word.

9. u s e f u l

10. h o p e f u l

11. r e s t f u l

12. h a r m f u l

13. f e a r f u l

14. h e l p f u l

15. p l a y f u l

16. c a r e f u l

What's that in the darkness?
A space monster in flight?
I'm almost fearless,
But I'll turn on the light!

Add **less** or **ness** to each base word.
Print the new word on the line. Use
the new words to finish the sentences.

RULE

You can add the ending **ness** or **less**
to a base word to make a new
word.

dark + ness = darkness
fear + less = fearless

less

1. use _____

2. sleep _____

3. harm _____

4. fear _____

ness

5. thick _____

6. dark _____

7. loud _____

8. sharp _____

9. It is _____ to tell me the bear is harmless.

10. I am not brave and _____.

11. When I think about the bear, I'm _____.

12. The bear's eyes are glowing in the _____.

13. The _____ of its snarls worries me.

14. I can almost feel the _____ of its teeth.

15. I see the _____ of its strong legs.

Lesson 75
Suffixes -less, -ness

Home

Write base words and suffixes on
separate cards and have your child
match them.

Name _____

Slowly the sun rises.
Quickly the sky gets bright.
Slowly the sun will set again,
When it's nearly night.

▶ Add **the ending ly to each base word.**
Print the new word on the line.

1. glad _____

2. swift _____

3. soft _____

4. brave _____

5. loud _____

6. slow _____

7. love _____

8. near _____

▶ Circle **each ly ending in the sentences. Print the base**
words on the lines.

9. Tigers walk softly.   _____

10. Lions roar bravely.   _____

11. Monkeys screech loudly.   _____

12. Turtles crawl slowly.   _____

13. Deer run swiftly.   _____

14. I watch them at the
    zoo gladly.   _____

15. The zoo near my house
    is lovely.   _____

Match the base word in the first column with the new word in the second column. **Print the letter on the line.**

1

_____ quick   **a.** slowly

_____ sweet   **b.** quickly

_____ slow   **c.** sweetly

_____ loud   **d.** loudly

_____ nice   **e.** nicely

2

_____ glad   **a.** softly

_____ soft   **b.** nearly

_____ near   **c.** lovely

_____ love   **d.** gladly

_____ brave   **e.** bravely

3

_____ use   **a.** playful

_____ play   **b.** handful

_____ cheer   **c.** useful

_____ hand   **d.** harmful

_____ harm   **e.** cheerful

4

_____ care   **a.** fearless

_____ sleeve   **b.** helpless

_____ fear   **c.** jobless

_____ job   **d.** careless

_____ help   **e.** sleeveless

5

_____ home   **a.** sleepless

_____ sleep   **b.** cheerless

_____ use   **c.** homeless

_____ wire   **d.** useless

_____ cheer   **e.** wireless

6

_____ good   **a.** softness

_____ dark   **b.** sadness

_____ kind   **c.** darkness

_____ sad   **d.** goodness

_____ soft   **e.** kindness

Review suffixes -ly, -ful, -less, -ness

Home

With your child, think of other words to add to the boxes.

Name _____

▶ **Add** an ending from the box to finish the word in each sentence. **Print** it on the line. **Trace** the whole word.

ly
ful
less
ness

1. Polly was usually brave and _fear_____.

2. Today she was _lone_____ in her new school.

3. She thought of her old friends with _sad_____.

4. She remembered all their _kind_____.

5. _Sudden_____ she saw some girls smiling at her.

6. Now she felt more _cheer_____.

▶ **Read** the words in the box. **Print** each word next to its definition.

7. with no fear _____

8. full of play _____

9. in a safe way _____

10. being dark _____

fearless
darkness
safely
playful

Say and spell the words in the tic-tac-toe grids. Follow the directions for each grid. Draw straight lines through three words across, up and down, or on a diagonal to win.

1 Match **ly** words.

blasting	sunless	lovely
stars	biggest	slowly
hopeful	roared	nicely

2 Match **ness** words.

darkness	cheerful	sweetly
longest	softness	rockets
fearful	stronger	coldness

3 Match **ful** words.

warmly	swiftness	joyful
smarter	joined	trying
careful	helpful	wishful

4 Match **less** words.

kindness	careless	playful
nearly	moonless	starting
lighter	fearless	quickly

166

Lesson 77
Review Suffixes -ly, -ful, -less, -ness

Home

Ask your child to read aloud the words that won each tic-tac-toe game.

Name _____

That star on the left is very bright,
But the brighter star is on the right.
Which are the brightest stars of all,
The ones in the sky or the ones that fall?

▶ **Add** the ending **er** and **est** to each word. **Print** the new words on the lines.

er   **est**

1. near _____   _____

2. long _____   _____

3. fast _____   _____

4. dark _____   _____

5. thick _____   _____

6. deep _____   _____

7. soft _____   _____

▶ **Draw** a picture to show the meaning of each word.

8

9

10

long   longer   longest

Lesson 78
Suffixes -er, -est

Finish each sentence by adding **er** or **est** to each base word.
Use **er** to tell about two things. Use **est** to tell about more
than two things. Print the new word on the line.

1. tall 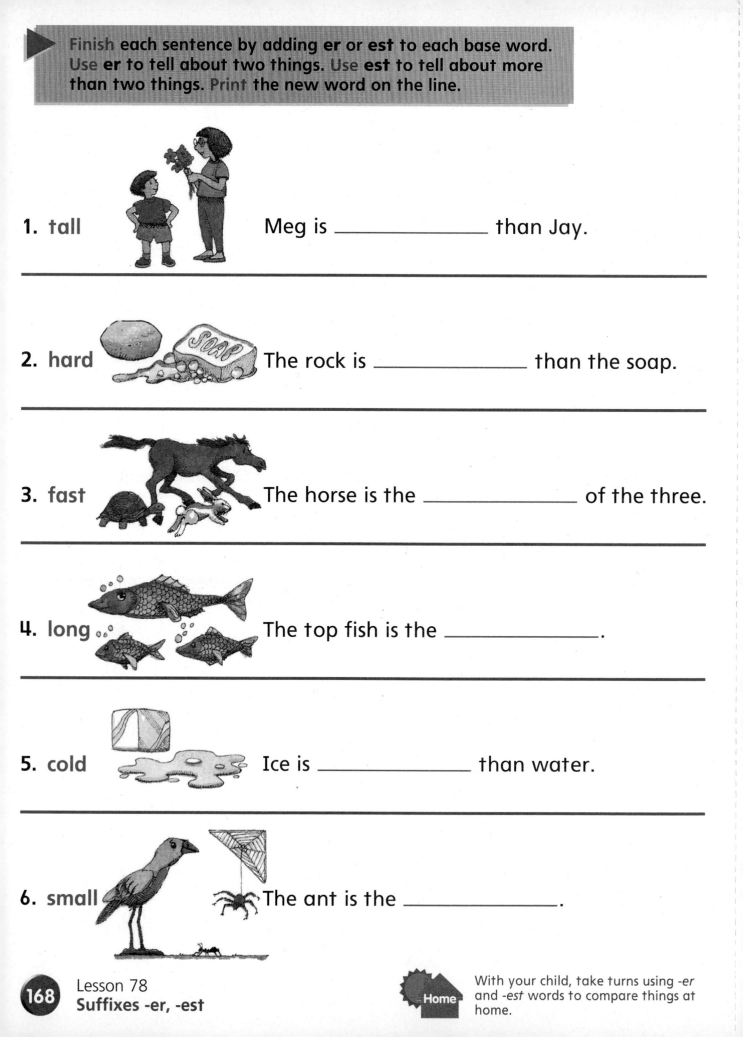 Meg is _____ than Jay.

2. hard The rock is _____ than the soap.

3. fast The horse is the _____ of the three.

4. long The top fish is the _____.

5. cold Ice is _____ than water.

6. small The ant is the _____.

Lesson 78
Suffixes -er, -est

With your child, take turns using -er
and -est words to compare things at
home.

Home

Name _____

Add **er** and **est** to each word.
Print the new words on the lines.

er   **est**

1. silly   _____   _____

2. happy _____   _____

3. windy _____   _____

4. fluffy _____   _____

Finish each sentence by adding **er** or **est** to the base word in the box.

5. Today was Justin's _____ day of the week.

| happy |

6. He got to the bus stop _____ than he did yesterday.

| early |

7. It was _____ than it had been all week.

| sunny |

8. He made up the _____ joke he could.

| silly |

9. The other kids said it was the

_____ one they had heard.

| funny |

Lesson 79
Suffixes -er, -est: words ending in y

▶ **Circle the name of each picture.**

RULE
When a word ends in **y** after a consonant, change the **y** to **i** before adding **es**.
story + es = stories

1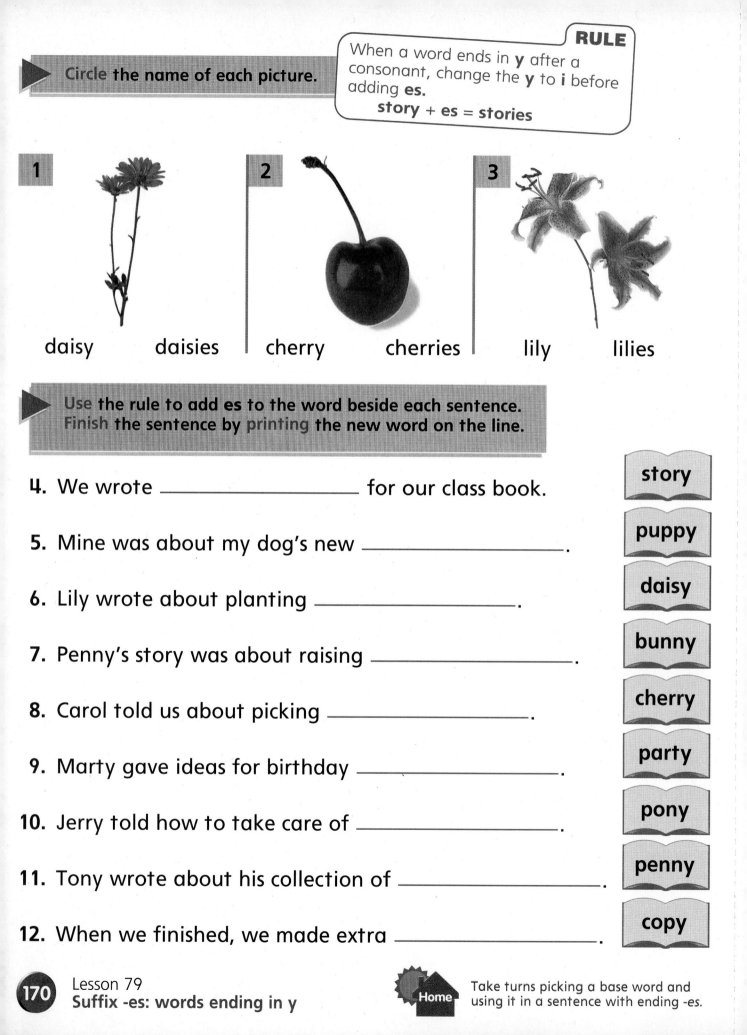

daisy   daisies

2

cherry   cherries

3

lily   lilies

▶ **Use the rule to add es to the word beside each sentence. Finish the sentence by printing the new word on the line.**

4. We wrote _____ for our class book.

5. Mine was about my dog's new _____.

6. Lily wrote about planting _____.

7. Penny's story was about raising _____.

8. Carol told us about picking _____.

9. Marty gave ideas for birthday _____.

10. Jerry told how to take care of _____.

11. Tony wrote about his collection of _____.

12. When we finished, we made extra _____.

story

puppy

daisy

bunny

cherry

party

pony

penny

copy

Home
Take turns picking a base word and using it in a sentence with ending -es.

Name _____

1	bunny	**2**	city	**3**	box
_____		_____		_____	
4	lily	**5**	dress	**6**	pony
_____		_____		_____	

▶ Circle the word that will finish each sentence. Print it on the line. Then print the name of each picture below.

7. Mary's birthday _____ was fun.   party   parties

8. Her dad read scary _____.   story   stories

9. We tossed _____ into bottles.   penny   pennies

10. Instead of cake, we ate _____ pie.   cherry   cherries

11. We got little _____ to take home.   candy   candies

12	**13**	**14**
_____	_____	_____

1. Farms are different from _____.

2. Sometimes my friends and our _____ visit a farm.

3. Sometimes there are lots of _____ in the fields.

4. Some _____ grow by the streams.

5. We like to ride the _____.

6. There are many different animal _____.

7. It's fun to play with the _____.

8. We usually see some _____.

9. Apples and _____ grow on farms.

10. We climb trees to pick _____.

11. I like to write _____ about our trips to the country.

12. I give _____ to my friends to read.

city

family

daisy

lily

pony

baby

bunny

puppy

berry

cherry

story

copy

Where does the family in the story live?

Home

Write words from the list above and have your child write the plural by changing *y* to *i* and adding *-es*.

Name _____

Print the word next to the comet with the same ending.
Print two contractions next to the last comet.

Word List

coldness	going	can't	thoughtful	lovely	funnier
blasted	waiting	darkness	deepest	glasses	bushes
happiest	wanted	slowly	careful	brighter	they're

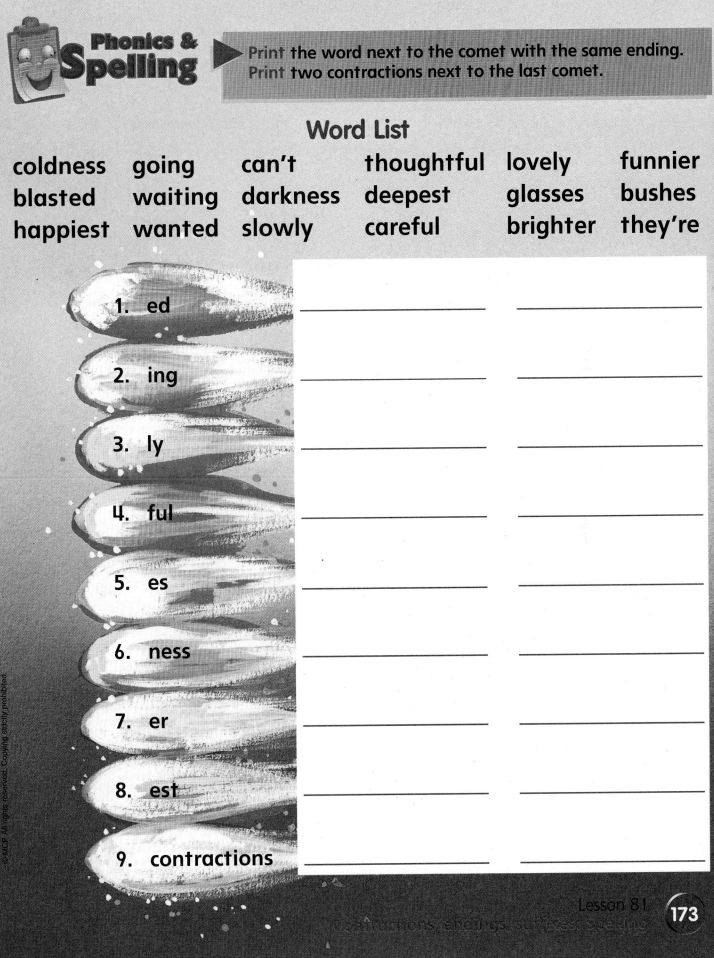

1. ed _____ _____

2. ing _____ _____

3. ly _____ _____

4. ful _____ _____

5. es _____ _____

6. ness _____ _____

7. er _____ _____

8. est _____ _____

9. contractions _____ _____

Contractions, endings, suffixes: Spelling

You are the first person to ever walk on the moon. Make a sign telling who you are, where you're from, and why you are on the moon. Use the words below to write your sign.

faster	longest	can't	careful	darkness
it's	wanted	waiting	earlier	wishes
useful	happiest	stories	I'll	bravely

Lesson 81
Contractions, endings, suffixes: Writing

Home

Ask your child to read words in the letter that have the endings listed on page 173.

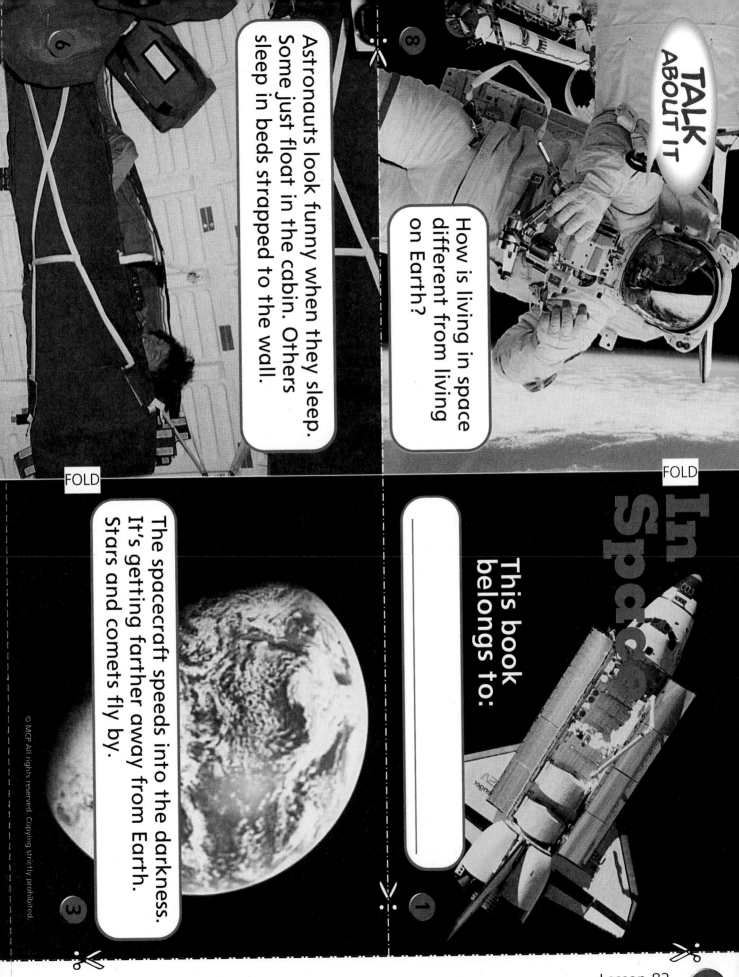

6

Astronauts look funny when they sleep. Some just float in the cabin. Others sleep in beds strapped to the wall.

FOLD

8

How is living in space different from living on Earth?

FOLD

3

The spacecraft speeds into the darkness. It's getting farther away from Earth. Stars and comets fly by.

In Space

This book belongs to:

1

When their work is finished, the astronauts have time to play.

FOLD

Eating in space can be tricky. Hold onto your lunch or it will float away!

FOLD

The spacecraft blasts off. It soars quickly into the cloudless sky. Leaving a white trail, it climbs higher and higher.

In space, everything is weightless. It's hard to keep your feet on the ground.

Lesson 82
Review contractions, endings, suffixes: Take-Home Book

Name _____

Fill in the bubble beside the word that names or describes each picture.

1
○ box
○ socks
○ boxes

2
○ fishing
○ sleeping
○ runs

3
○ glass
○ guess
○ glasses

4
○ puppy
○ ponies
○ puppies

5
○ daisy
○ daisies
○ days

6
○ dish
○ ditches
○ dishes

7
○ star
○ stars
○ start

8
○ peaches
○ peach
○ beach

9
○ mailed
○ nails
○ sailed

10
○ baked
○ cook
○ back

11
○ raking
○ baking
○ jumped

12
○ racing
○ reading
○ walked

Contractions, endings, suffixes: Checkup

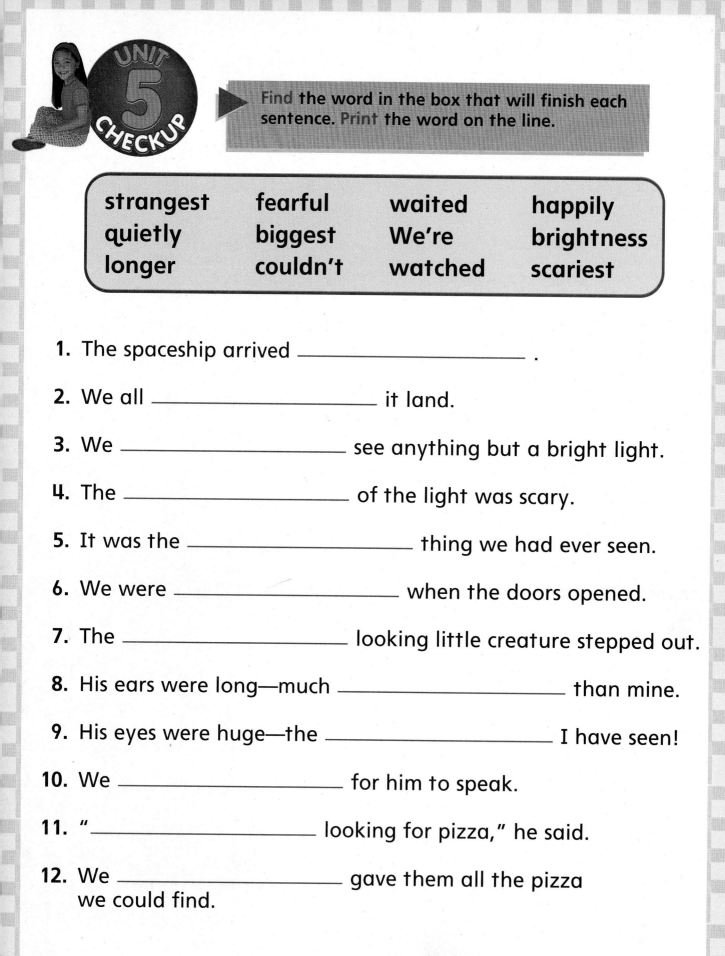

Find the word in the box that will finish each sentence. Print the word on the line.

strangest	fearful	waited	happily
quietly	biggest	We're	brightness
longer	couldn't	watched	scariest

1. The spaceship arrived _____ .

2. We all _____ it land.

3. We _____ see anything but a bright light.

4. The _____ of the light was scary.

5. It was the _____ thing we had ever seen.

6. We were _____ when the doors opened.

7. The _____ looking little creature stepped out.

8. His ears were long—much _____ than mine.

9. His eyes were huge—the _____ I have seen!

10. We _____ for him to speak.

11. "_____ looking for pizza," he said.

12. We _____ gave them all the pizza we could find.

 Home   Ask your child to read the story on this page and think of a title for it.

DINOSAUR MUSEUM

Apatosaurus, Stegosaurus,
Tyrannosaurus rex.
There are so many dinosaur bones,
What will we see next?

Long tails, huge feet,
Sharp teeth with which to chew.
What do you think they really looked like?
I only wish we knew.

Look at all these dinosaur bones!
They reach from head to toe!
But how they lived and what they saw,
I guess we'll never know.

▶ Describe what you think dinosaurs looked like.

THINK! Why do you think people search for dinosaur bones?

Home Letter

Dear Family,

In the next few weeks we'll be learning about vowel pairs, digraphs, and diphthongs while we explore the wonderful world of dinosaurs.

At-Home Activities

Here are some activities you and your child can do together.

▶ Make a clay model of a dinosaur. Ask your child to identify the parts of the animal and write them down together. Circle words with vowel pairs, digraphs, and diphthongs, such as tail, head, toes, teeth, and mouth.

▶ Look in the library for books about dinosaurs. As you read, point out words that have different vowel sounds, such as round, brown, pool, and coat.

Book Corner

You and your child might enjoy reading these books together. Look for them in your local library.

Holding Onto Sunday
by Kathryn O. Galbraith

One Sunday, Jemma and her father go dinosaur hunting at the museum.

Discovering Dinosaur Babies
by Miriam Schleir

How dinosaurs lived and raised their families, based on recent discoveries of dinosaur eggs, is explained in this fascinating book.

Sincerely,

Name _____

Gail said, "What a rainy day!
Another rainy Saturday!
Let's stay right here and play.
Let's make dinosaurs from clay."

▶ Find **the word in the box that names
each picture.** Print **it on the line.**

RULE

In a **vowel pair,** two vowels come
together to make one long vowel
sound. The first vowel stands for
the long sound and the second
vowel is silent. You can hear the
long **a** sound in **rainy** and **day.**

sail	pay	rain	tail	hay
tray	spray	chain	nail	

1 _____

2 _____

3 _____

4 _____

5 _____

6 _____

7 _____

8 _____

9 _____

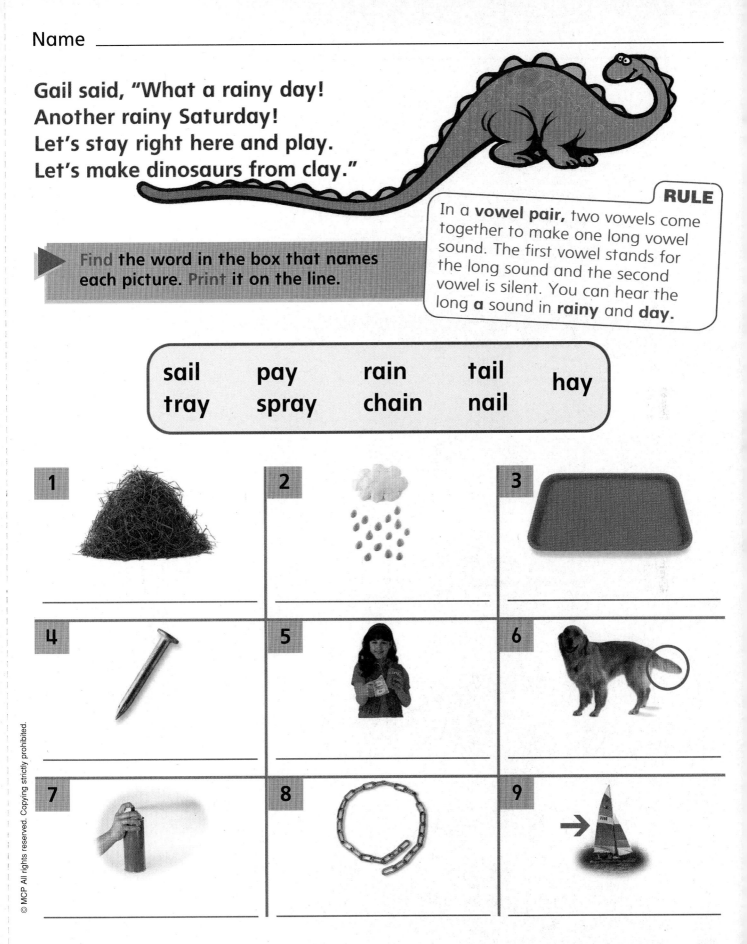

Lesson 84
Vowel pairs ai, ay

chain	stain	mailbox	hay	pail	rain	tray
hair	paint	chair	train	gray	sail	day

1. I ride on railroad tracks. _____

2. You put letters in me. _____

3. I am a blend of black and white. _____

4. If I start, you put on a raincoat. _____

5. You can sit on me. _____

6. I am made of many links. _____

7. I am part of a boat. _____

8. I am an ink spot on a shirt. _____

9. I am piled in a stack. _____

10. You can use a comb on me. _____

11. You can carry water in me. _____

12. I am spread on a wall. _____

13. You carry food on me. _____

14. I come before night. _____

Lesson 84
Vowel pairs ai, ay: Words in context

Home

With your child, take turns using
each word in the box in a sentence.

Name _____

Circle the name of each picture.

1
sell
seal
seed

2
bean
bed
bee

3
jeep
jeans
peep

4
leaf
lean
leak

5
jeeps
jeans
jets

6
feed
feet
feel

7
deep
deeds
deer

8
meat
met
team

9
eat
each
ear

10
peach
peace
pear

11
seal
seed
send

12
team
test
teeth

keep	eager	easy	meal
feet	steer	beaver	each
teeth	leaves	seem	seen

1. Have you ever _____ a beaver? _____

2. A _____ likes to chew down trees. _____

3. It makes a _____ of the bark. _____

4. It uses _____ branch to build a dam. _____

5. It only _____ the stump behind. _____

6. A beaver's _____ have to be strong. _____

7. Its webbed _____ help it swim along. _____

8. It uses its tail to _____. _____

9. It's not _____ being a beaver. _____

10. Beavers always _____ to be working. _____

11. They _____ working until all their work is done. _____

12. That's why busy people are often called

" _____ beavers." _____

THINK! Why is the beaver so busy?

Home   Help your child sort the words according to vowel pairs (ea or ee).

Name _____

RULE

▶ **Circle the word that will finish each sentence. Print it on the line.**

1. My friend, _____, and I went to the store.

jay
Joe
jot

2. Along the way, we saw a _____ by the road.

die
doe
day

3. When we got there, Joe stubbed his _____.

tie
toe
lie

4. My dog _____ stayed outside.

Moe
my
mine

5. I wanted to buy a new red _____.

tie
toe
lie

6. We all had some _____ when we got home.

pie
pine
pile

THINK! **Why did Moe stay outside?**

Lesson 86
Vowel pairs ie, oe: Words in context

185

RULE

The vowel pair **ow** sometimes has the long **o** sound. The vowel pair **oa** has the long **o** sound. You can hear the long **o** sound in **bowl** and **boat**.

boat   rainbow   goat   bow   soap   bowl

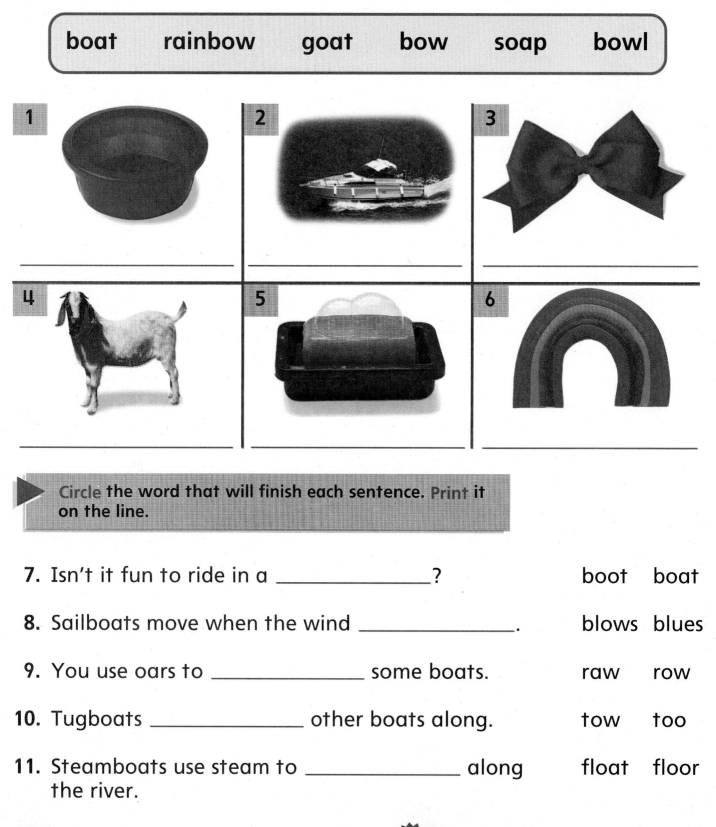

1 _____

2 _____

3 _____

4 _____

5 _____

6 _____

Circle the word that will finish each sentence. **Print** it on the line.

7. Isn't it fun to ride in a _____?   boot   boat

8. Sailboats move when the wind _____.   blows   blues

9. You use oars to _____ some boats.   raw   row

10. Tugboats _____ other boats along.   tow   too

11. Steamboats use steam to _____ along   float   floor
    the river.

 Home

Have your child circle the vowel pairs *oa* and *ow* in the words on this page.

Phonics & Reading

▶ **Read** the story. **Print** a word with a vowel pair on the line to finish each sentence.

Kay's Surprise

One day Kay's Aunt Jean sent her a surprise—a pet iguana. Kay had never seen anything like it.

It looked like a baby dinosaur. It had a brown and green coat and a long tail. It also had big feet with a sharp little claw on each toe.

Kay got a book about iguanas to read. She learned that iguanas don't eat meat. They need a meal of lettuce once a day. They also like sweet potatoes, apples and oranges. Iguanas need to stay warm and like to lie in the sun. They can also grow to be six feet long!

1. It had a brown and green _____ and a long _____

2. Iguanas need a _____ of lettuce once a _____.

3. They also like _____ potatoes.

 Would an iguana make a good pet? Why or why not?

Pretend you are Kay. Write a note to Aunt Jean to thank her for the surprise. Use some of the words in the box.

neat
toe
sweet
lie
bow
teeth
tail
know
seen
wait

Dear _____

_____

_____

_____

_____

_____

_____

_____

                            _____

Lesson 87
Review vowel pairs: Writing

Home

Have your child circle the vowel pairs in the words in *Kay's Surprise*.

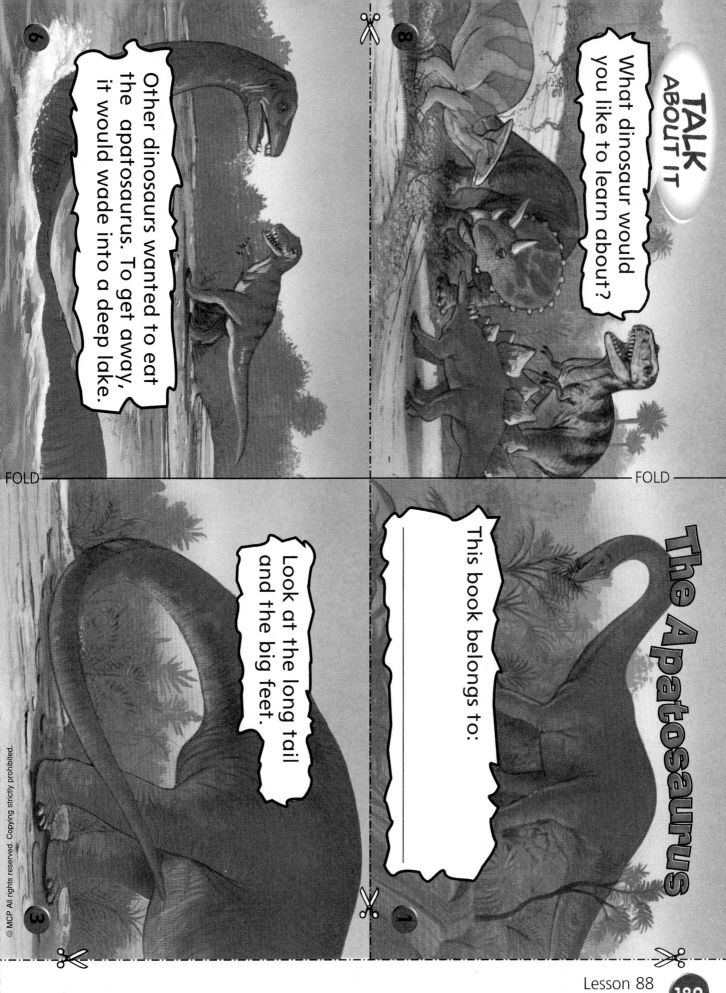

6

Other dinosaurs wanted to eat the apatosaurus. To get away, it would wade into a deep lake.

3

Look at the long tail and the big feet.

8

TALK ABOUT IT

What dinosaur would you like to learn about?

This book belongs to:

_____

The Apatosaurus

1

Lesson 88
Review vowel pairs: Take-Home Book

The apatosaurus would soak in the lake and eat water plants for hours. For an animal with a small brain, it was very smart.

The apatosaurus had to eat many meals every day. It liked to pull leaves off trees and eat them.

FOLD

FOLD

This is an apatosaurus. This dinosaur had a little brain, but a giant body.

2

From head to tail, the apatosaurus could grow 90 feet long. It was 30 feet high.

4

Lesson 88
Review vowel pairs: Take-Home Book

Name _____

A tooth here, a foot bone, too.
We use tools to dig and brush.
When you look for dinosaur bones,
You can't be in a rush.

RULE

In a **vowel digraph,** two vowels together can make a long or a short sound, or have a special sound all their own. You can hear the different sounds of the vowel digraph **oo** in **tooth** and **foot.**

▶ Circle **the word that will finish each sentence. Print** it on the line.

broom
loose

1. I felt something _____ in my mouth.

_____

tool
tooth

2. Was it a _____?

_____

room
zoo

3. I ran to my _____.

_____

spoon
stool

4. I stood on a _____ to look in the mirror.

_____

moon
soon

5. My tooth should fall out _____.

_____

soon
noon

6. At _____ it was time for lunch.

_____

food
fool

7. I took a bite of _____ with my spoon.

_____

soothe
spoon

8. Out came my loose tooth on the _____.

_____

too
zoo

9. My friend lost a tooth, _____.

_____

 **THINK!** **Why do you lose your teeth?**

> **Find** a word in the box that will finish each sentence. **Print** it on the line.

cookie	look	good	stood
book	cook	took	hook

1. I was looking for a good _____.

2. I took a _____ at a cookbook.

3. I _____ in line to pay for the book.

4. Then I _____ my new book home.

5. I decided to _____ something.

6. I took my apron off a _____.

7. I tried a _____ recipe.

8. The cookies were very _____.

> **Print** the missing letters of each picture's name. **Print** the missing letters for a word that **rhymes** with it. **Trace** the whole word.

9
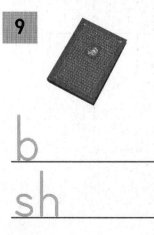
b _____
sh _____

10
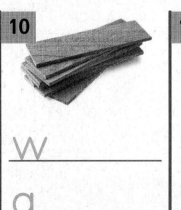
w _____
g _____

11

h _____
br _____

12

h _____
st _____

Lesson 89
Vowel digraph oo

Home With your child, make up a rhyme for each pair of words above.

Name _____

RULE
The vowel digraph **ea** can stand for the short **e** sound. You can hear the short **e** sound in **ready**.

ahead	already	breakfast	spread
bread	breath	head	

1. When you wake up, take a deep _____.

2. It will help clear your _____.

3. Now you are ready for _____.

4. Here is some _____ to make toast.

5. You can _____ butter and jam on it.

6. The eggs are _____ made.

7. Go _____ and eat.

Circle the correct word to finish each sentence.

8. What is the (feather, weather, leather) like today?

9. Will you need to wear a (sweater, weather, meadow)?

10. Maybe you will need a (ready, heavy, cleanser) coat.

11. Is it cold enough for (bread, thread, leather) boots?

12. Cover your (head, heavy, breakfast) with a warm hat.

13. Now you are (meadow, heavy, ready) to go outside.

1

seat
bread
meat
bean

2

bread
beach
heavy
treat

3

reach
steam
break
great

4

dream
mean
beak
health

5

head
heavy
lean
steak

6

steak
tea
teacher
great

7

beaver
team
leather
beans

8

bread
weather
seal
leather

9

ready
heavy
bread
bean

10

beach
teach
health
reach

11

break
leather
thread
weather

12

meat
great
heat
leak

194 Lesson 90
Vowel digraph ea

With your child, take turns naming a word that rhymes with each picture name.

Name _____

Lesson 91

Find **the word in the box that will**
finish each sentence. Print **it on**
the line.

RULE
The vowel digraphs **au** and **aw** usually
have the same sound. You
can hear the sound of **au** and **aw**
in **August** and **paw.**

drawing	autumn	straws	haul	August
lawn	pause	yawn	crawls	Paula

1. _____ is a lazy month.

2. We _____ in our work to relax.

3. _____ and I play games in the shade.

4. I water the _____ in the evenings.

5. We _____ the picnic basket to the lake.

6. After swimming, we _____ and nap in the sun.

7. We sip lemonade through _____.

8. My baby brother _____ on the grass.

9. Summer's end is _____ near.

10. Soon _____ will come, and school will start.

THINK! **Why does this family**
like August?

fawns

draw

because

pause

Paul

hawk

crawl

paws

1. _____ likes to draw.

2. He draws and draws without a _____.

3. He can _____ animals that look real.

4. Paul can make a _____ that has
sharp claws.

5. His turtles almost seem to _____.

6. He draws dogs with huge _____.

7. He draws _____ hiding in trees.

8. Paul draws so well _____ he
practices a lot.

THINK! How do you know Paul likes to draw?

Home

Have your child write the words on
pages 195-196 with the letters au and
aw.

Name _____

Read the words in the bubbles. Print each word under the picture that has the same vowel sound.

cook
broom
hook
head
yawn
claw
pool
break
bread
leaf
team

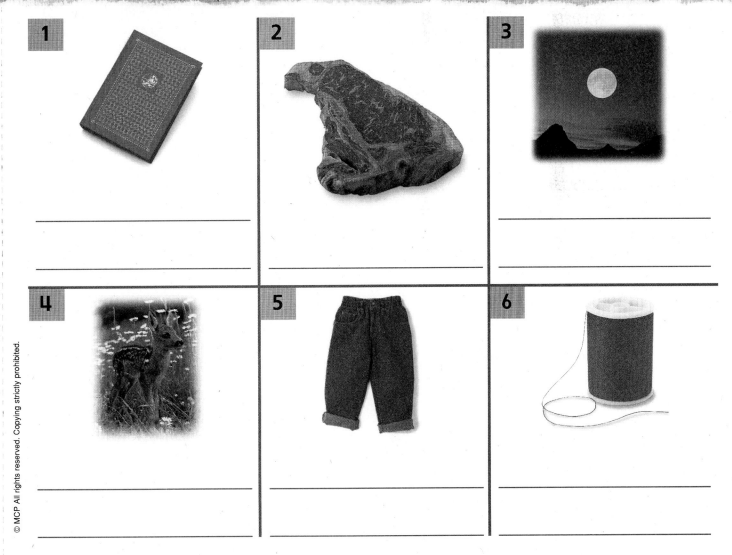

1

_____
_____

2

_____
_____

3

_____
_____

4

_____
_____

5

_____
_____

6

_____
_____

Say the name of each picture. Circle the letters that stand for the vowel sound in the picture's name. Then print the letters to finish its name. Trace the whole word.

1
aw
oo
ea

s ___

2
aw
ea
oo

br ___ d

3
aw
oo
ea

f ___ ther

4
ea
au
oo

sp ___ n

5
oo
ea
aw

st ___ k

6
au
ea
oo

p ___ l

7
(oo)
au
ea

w ___ d

8
aw
oo
ea

str ___

9
ea
aw
oo

f ___ n

10
aw
ea
oo

j ___ ns

11
ea
oo
au

l ___ ndry

12
oo
ea
aw

wh ___ t

Lesson 92
Review vowel digraphs oo, ea, au, aw

Home

Have your child circle the digraphs in the words on page 197.

Name _____

Phonics & Reading

▶ Read the newspaper article. Print a word with **oo, ea, au,** or **aw** from the story on the line to finish each sentence.

What Really Happened?

Long ago, the heavy feet of giant dinosaurs shook the earth. Then something awful happened. All of these awesome animals died. Scientists are looking for clues to find out what really happened.

Some scientists think a meteor or comet hit the earth, causing great fires. Dust and ash blocked the sun's light and changed the weather. Warm places became cool. Cool places became colder. Plants and small animals died because of the cold. The dinosaurs could not find food.

1. Their _____ feet _____ the earth.

2. A comet may have hit the earth, _____ great fires.

3. These _____ animals died.

THINK! **Why do you think the dinosaurs died?**

Lesson 93
Digraphs oo, ea, au, aw: Reading

Pretend that you have discovered some dinosaur bones. Write a story for your school newspaper to tell people about your discovery. Use some of the words in the box.

claw	book	heavy	paws	taught
head	draw	because	look	jaw

200
Lesson 93
Review digraphs oo, ea, au, aw: Writing

Home

Ask your child to use each of the words in the box in a sentence.

6

Then he saw a huge mouth full of sharp teeth! The thing tried to snap Dean up in its jaws!

8

TALK ABOUT IT

How do you think Mother Dinosaur would feel if she knew about Dean's day out?

FOLD

FOLD

3

Dean stuck his head out of the shell. Then he crawled out of the egg and looked around.

1

This book belongs to:

DEAN'S DAY OUT

7

Dean crawled back into his shell. Mother Dinosaur came back and saw him. "What a good boy!" she said. "You can come out now."

5

A mean-looking thing flew down. It tried to catch Dean in its beak! Dean hid under a leaf.

FOLD

FOLD

Mother Dinosaur tapped each egg. "Not ready yet," she said. "I'll go look for some good green leaves to eat."

2

Everything was new to Dean. He set out to see the world.

4

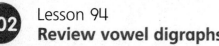

202

Lesson 94
Review vowel digraphs: Take-Home Book

Name _____

Dino sleeps outside the house.
He never makes a sound.
He doesn't eat the flowers.
He's the greatest pet in town.

Say **the name of the picture.** Find **its name in the list.** Print **its letter on the line below the picture.**

RULE

A **diphthong** is made up of two letters blended together to make one sound. You can hear the sound of the diphthongs **ou** and **ow** in **house** and **flowers.**

1

_____

2

_____

3

_____

4

_____

a. clown   h. crown

b. cowboy   i. cloud

c. mouse   j. cow

d. shower   k. towel

e. howl   l. flowers

f. owl   m. house

g. now   n. mouth

5

_____

6

_____

7

_____

8

_____

9

_____

10

_____

1. I live on the edge of a small town. _____

2. My house is near a farm. _____

3. I spend a lot of time outdoors. _____

4. From my yard I can see cows and horses. _____

5. In the summer I watch the farmer plow his field. _____

6. His tractor makes a loud noise. _____

7. At night, I hear many different sounds. _____

8. I can hear owls calling. _____

9. I like to watch the clouds beyond the hills. _____

10. In the fall the flowers on the hill bloom. _____

11. Today I saw a flock of birds flying south. _____

12. They sense that winter is about to start. _____

Does the person in the story live in the city or the country?

Name _____

owl	flower	house	plow
cow	cloud	clown	ground

1 I am in the sky.
Sometimes I bring you rain.
What am I?

_____

2 I wear a funny suit.
I do many tricks.
I can make you smile.
What am I?

_____

3 I am in the garden.
I am very colorful.
I may grow in your yard,
too.

_____

4 You can plant seeds in me.
The farmer must plow me.
What am I?

_____

5 I am wide awake in the dark.
I hoot and howl.
What am I?

_____

6 You can see me at the farm.
I eat green grass.
I give you good milk.
What am I?

_____

7 You can live in me.
I will keep you warm
and cozy.
What am I?

_____

8 The farmer uses me.
I help him make his garden.
What am I?

_____

Print an X beside each word in which **ow** stands for the long **o** sound.

1. ____ how
2. ____ snow
3. ____ own
4. ____ town

5. ____ crowd
6. ____ now
7. ____ bowl
8. ____ grow

9. ____ low
10. ____ plow
11. ____ power
12. ____ owl

13. ____ slow
14. ____ flow
15. ____ know
16. ____ show

17. ____ brown
18. ____ crow
19. ____ crown
20. ____ down

21. ____ towel
22. ____ glow
23. ____ throw
24. ____ brown

25. ____ cow
26. ____ blow
27. ____ arrow
28. ____ tower

Circle the **ow** word in each sentence. **Print** an X in the correct column to show which sound **ow** makes.

	long vowel	diphthong
29. The circus came to our town.	____	____
30. We went to the show last night.	____	____
31. We sat in the very first row.	____	____
32. The star was a funny clown.	____	____
33. He made the crowd laugh.	____	____

 Home

Help your child make cards for words 1–10 and sort them according to the long o sound.

Name _____

RULE

Circle **the name of each picture.**

The diphthongs **oi** and **oy** usually stand for the same sound. You can hear that sound in **coin** and **boy.**

1

bow
boil
bill

2

boy
bag
toy

3

corn
coil
coins

4

sail
sell
soil

5

oak
oil
out

6

toil
tail
toys

7

paint
point
pail

8

noise
nail
nose

9

fame
foil
fawn

Finish **each sentence with a word from the box.**

enjoy   toy   coins

10. I have saved a few dollars and some _____.

11. I will buy a _____ robot kit.

12. I will _____ putting it together.

The Runaway Toy

A boy named Roy had a birthday. His grandmother and grandfather gave him a choice of toys. Roy chose a toy train. He was a very happy boy.

Roy enjoyed his toy train, but it made too much noise. Roy took out a can of oil and oiled the toy. The oil made the train less noisy. It made it go faster, too.

One day Roy oiled it too much. The train went faster and faster. It raced around the room and out the door. Roy chased it. The toy train rolled up to his sister, Joy.

"Look," said Joy. "This toy wants to join me outside."

"That's my toy train," said Roy. "It ran away from me. From now on I will be more careful. I will not spoil my toy with too much oil."

Use the words you marked to answer the questions.

1. What was the boy's name?   _____

2. What kind of train did he get?   _____

3. What made the train go fast?   _____

4. What made Roy oil the train?   _____

THINK! **What other toys could Roy have chosen?**

 Together, read and act out the story. Then switch roles.

Name _____

▶ **Find** the word on the bowl that will finish each sentence. **Print** it on the line.

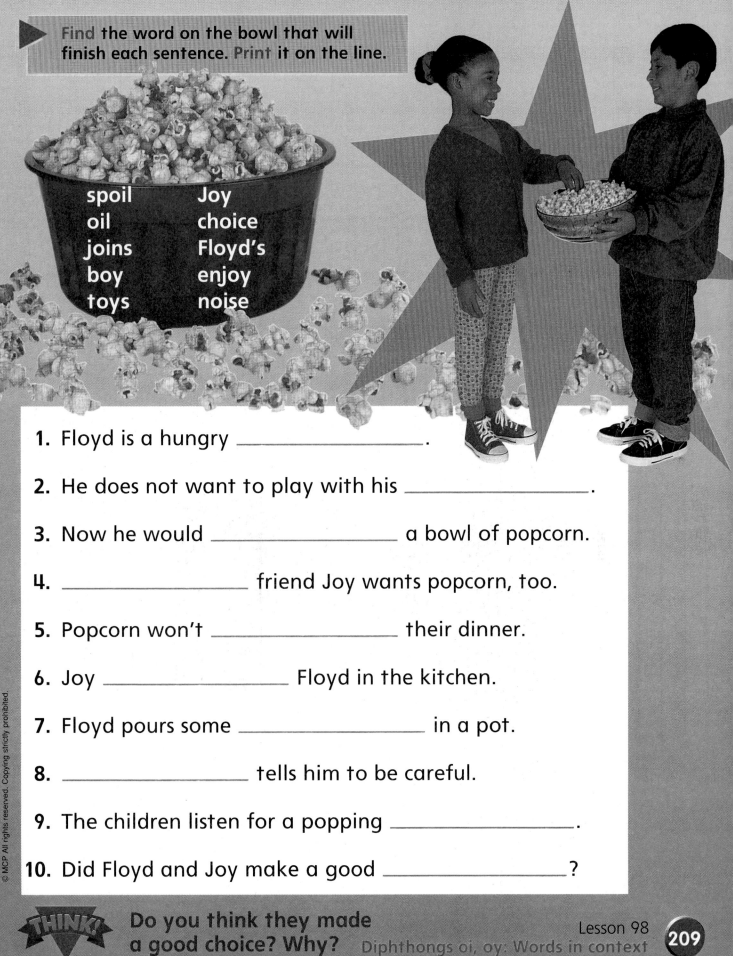

spoil Joy
oil choice
joins Floyd's
boy enjoy
toys noise

1. Floyd is a hungry _____.

2. He does not want to play with his _____.

3. Now he would _____ a bowl of popcorn.

4. _____ friend Joy wants popcorn, too.

5. Popcorn won't _____ their dinner.

6. Joy _____ Floyd in the kitchen.

7. Floyd pours some _____ in a pot.

8. _____ tells him to be careful.

9. The children listen for a popping _____.

10. Did Floyd and Joy make a good _____?

THINK! **Do you think they made a good choice? Why?** Diphthongs oi, oy: Words in context

1. Is a penny a coin? Yes No

2. Is joy being very sad? Yes No

3. Can you play with a toy? Yes No

4. Is oil used in a car? Yes No

5. Is a point the same as paint? Yes No

6. Can you boil water? Yes No

7. Can you make a choice? Yes No

8. Is a loud noise quiet? Yes No

► **Find the word in the box that will finish each sentence. Print it on the line.**

spoil
enjoys
toy
Joyce
noise
points
boy

9. _____ is glad the circus is in town.

10. She loves the _____ of the crowd.

11. The clown rides in a _____ cart.

12. She smiles and _____ at the funny clown.

13. She sees a _____ standing up on a horse.

14. Nothing can _____ the day for Joyce.

15. Joyce always _____ a day at the circus.

 Take turns using the *oi* and *oy* words in new sentences.

Name _____

▶ **Find** the word in the box that will finish each sentence. **Print** it on the line.

RULE

The diphthong **ew** stands for the long **u** sound. You can hear the long **u** sound in **new** and **few**.

grew
blew
chew
flew
new
threw
knew
few

1. I have a _____ pack of sugarless gum.

2. I put a _____ pieces into my mouth.

3. I began to _____ the gum.

4. Then I _____ a giant bubble.

5. That bubble grew and _____.

6. Suddenly, I _____ I was in trouble.

7. The bubble broke, and pieces _____ everywhere.

8. I _____ the pieces of chewed gum away.

▶ **Print** the missing letters for a word that **rhymes** with each word. **Trace** the whole word.

9 few	**10** crew	**11** grew
__st__	__thr__	__fl__

Circle the word that will finish each sentence.

1. (Drew, Blew, Knew) wanted a pet.

2. He went to a pet shop called (crew, dew, Flew) the Coop.

3. He saw puppies (chewing, stewing, mewing) on toy bones.

4. Baby birds (flew, stew, knew) around their cage.

5. They (few, threw, grew) seeds on the floor.

6. Drew really wanted a (mew, stew, new) kitten.

7. He saw a (chew, crew, grew) of kittens.

8. A (few, threw, grew) were very cute.

9. One kitten looked at him and (flew, mewed, chewed).

10. Drew (grew, dew, knew) he wanted that kitten.

11. Drew named him (Mews, Stews, Dews) because he always mewed.

12. That kitten (new, grew, chew) bigger every day.

13. Mews liked it when Drew (few, threw, mew) a toy to him.

14. He liked to (chew, new, stew) on Drew's shoestrings.

15. Mews tried to hide under the (screws, grew, newspaper).

16. From the window he watched birds as they (flew, crew, dew).

17. When the wind (blew, drew, stew), Mews chased fallen leaves.

18. He licked drops of morning (mew, dew, chew).

19. Before Drew (threw, few, knew) it, Mews was his friend.

20. Drew really loved his (stew, new, flew) pet.

What do you think Drew liked best about Mews?

Take turns reading every other line of the story.

Name _____

Phonics & Spelling

Say and spell the words in the box. Name each picture and write each word whose name has the same vowel sound. Then circle the letters that stand for the vowel sound.

cloud	hair	seed	wealth	lie	day
row	moon	draw	boy	soon	cow
tie	spoil	boat	peach	haul	head

1. _____
   _____

2. _____
   _____

3. _____
   _____

4. _____

5. _____
   _____

6. _____
   _____

7. _____
   _____

8. _____
   _____

9. _____

Lesson 100
Review vowel pairs, digraphs, diphthongs: Spelling

Phonics & Writing

Write a rhyme about dinosaurs. Use some of the words in the box. Share your rhyme with the class.

look	nail	sound	claw	know
ready	meat	found	toe	few
day	eat	green	die	new

Book Corner

Dinosaur Days
by Judy Nayer

Twins named Dawn and Paul share a love for dinosaurs, which continues even when they grow up.

Dinosaur Days
WRITTEN BY JUDY NAYER
ILLUSTRATED BY GAIL PIATZA

Home

Invite your child to read his or her poem aloud to family members.

Which dinosaur riddle do you like best? Why?

6

Answer: He followed the tracks!

How did the dinosaur find the missing train?

FOLD

FOLD

DINOSAUR RIDDLES

This book belongs to:

Why did the dinosaur throw the clock out the window?

3

Answer: He wanted to see time fly!

1

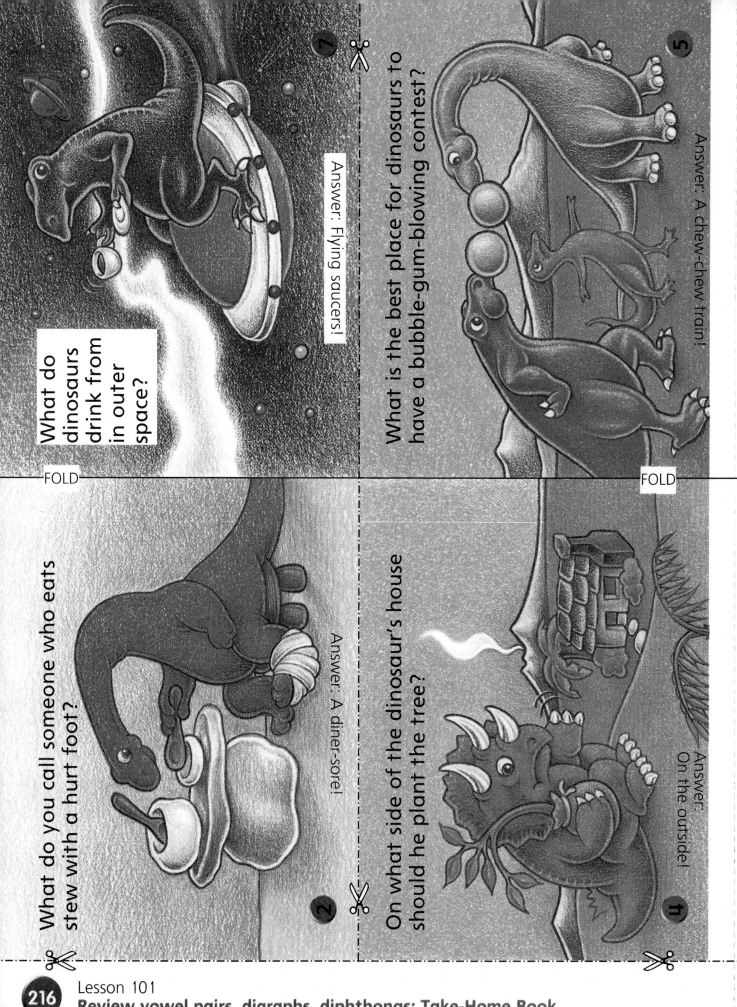

7

Answer: Flying saucers!

What do dinosaurs drink from in outer space?

FOLD

5

Answer: A chew-chew train!

What is the best place for dinosaurs to have a bubble-gum-blowing contest?

FOLD

What do you call someone who eats stew with a hurt foot?

Answer: A diner-sore!

2

On what side of the dinosaur's house should he plant the tree?

Answer: On the outside!

4

Name _____

Circle the word that will finish each sentence. Then print it on the line.

1. A baby deer is a _____.   seal   fawn   feather

2. A deep dish is a _____.   bean   bait   bowl

3. A place where you can see

   animals is a _____.   zoo   zipper hook

4. Dried grass that horses eat

   is _____.   seed   hay   day

5. A small animal with a long

   tail is a _____.   men   mitt   mouse

6. Something you row

   is a _____.   boat   beach   boy

7. You walk on your two

   _____.   feet   foot   flat

8. One animal that gives milk is

   a _____.   cloud   crow   cow

9. Something that was never

   used is _____.   grew   new   draw

10. A dish under a cup is a

   _____.   train   faucet saucer

Vowel pairs, digraphs, diphthongs: Checkup

Fill in the bubble in front of the word that will finish each sentence.

1. Dinosaurs ___ their eggs in nests. ○ day ○ laid ○ paid

2. The mother ___ around the eggs. ○ coiled ○ heated ○ boiled

3. Many dinosaurs ___ huge. ○ saw ○ drew ○ grew

4. The giant tyrannosaurus ate ___. ○ toys ○ meet ○ meat

5. It had long claws on each ___. ○ toe ○ foe ○ hair

6. It had sharp teeth in its ___. ○ bread ○ head ○ peach

7. It caught animals in its strong ___. ○ draw ○ jaw ○ haul

8. The stegosaurus had ___ of plates on its back. ○ rows ○ seeds ○ boats

9. It had bony spikes on its ___. ○ sail ○ coin ○ tail

10. No dinosaurs are alive ___. ○ cloud ○ now ○ cow

11. They ___ long ago. ○ died ○ lied ○ boy

12. We can only guess what they ___ like. ○ book ○ looked ○ playing

Lesson 102
Vowel pairs, digraphs, diphthongs: Checkup

Origami

Brightly colored squares,
Appearing, disappearing,
Lovely birds unfold.

 ▶ **Name the animals in the picture.**

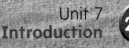 **How are the animals made?**

Home Letter

Dear Family,

In the next few weeks your child will be learning about different kinds of words, including

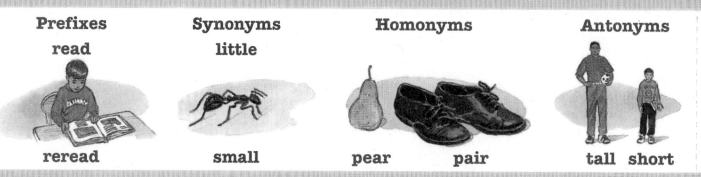

Prefixes	**Synonyms**	**Homonyms**	**Antonyms**
read	little		
reread	small	pear pair	tall short

As we learn new words we'll also be exploring a variety of different arts and crafts, such as origami, quilting, and making play dough.

At-Home Activities

Here are some activities you and your child can do together.

▶ Gather together uncooked spaghetti and macaroni, buttons, pieces of ribbon and yarn, and pictures cut from magazines. Help your child glue these items on paper to make a collage.

▶ Read the directions for a recipe. Together, look for words to which the prefixes **re, un,** and **dis** can be added to make new words—for example: **re**heat, **un**wrap, **dis**card.

Book Corner

You and your child might enjoy reading these books together.

The Keeping Quilt
by Patricia Polacco

This is the story of a special quilt made by the author's family. Each generation adds to the quilt using scraps of clothing.

I Can Draw Dinosaurs
by Toni Tallarico

Simple circles and squares turn into lifelike dinosaurs when children follow these easy step-by-step instructions.

Sincerely,

Name _____

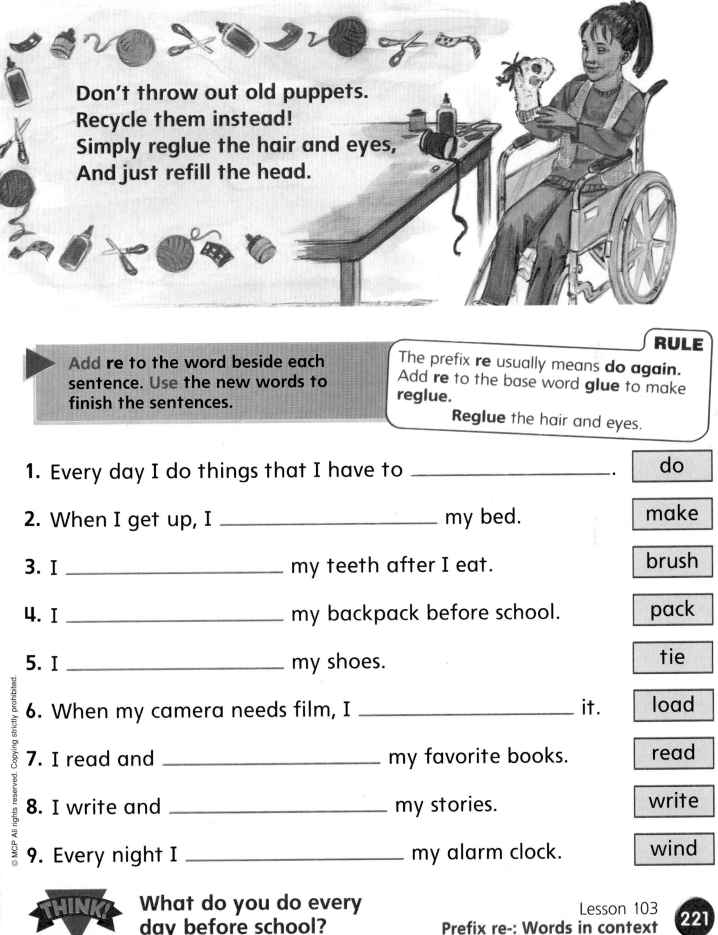

Don't throw out old puppets.
Recycle them instead!
Simply reglue the hair and eyes,
And just refill the head.

Add **re** to the word beside each sentence. **Use** the new words to finish the sentences.

RULE

The prefix **re** usually means **do again.** Add **re** to the base word **glue** to make **reglue.**

Reglue the hair and eyes.

1. Every day I do things that I have to _____. | do

2. When I get up, I _____ my bed. | make

3. I _____ my teeth after I eat. | brush

4. I _____ my backpack before school. | pack

5. I _____ my shoes. | tie

6. When my camera needs film, I _____ it. | load

7. I read and _____ my favorite books. | read

8. I write and _____ my stories. | write

9. Every night I _____ my alarm clock. | wind

THINK! **What do you do every day before school?**

Add un to the word beside each sentence. Use the new words to finish the sentences.

1. Every day we do things and _____ them. | do

2. We dress and _____. | dress

3. We button and _____ our clothes. | button

4. We tie our shoes and then _____ them. | tie

5. We lock and _____ doors. | lock

6. We buckle our seat belts and _____ them. | buckle

7. We wrap up our lunches and then

_____ them. | wrap

8. We pack our backpacks and _____ them. | pack

9. We load film in a camera and later _____ it. | load

10. I am not _____ about all this undoing. | happy

11. It just seems a little _____ to me. | usual

12. But it's probably _____ things will ever change. | likely

Lesson 103
Prefix un-: Words in context

With your child, take turns making up new sentences for the *un-* words.

Name _____

▶ Add **re** or **un** to the word beside each sentence. Use the new word to finish the sentence.

1. Last night my baby sister _____ my backpack.

   | packed |

2. She tried to _____ my homework with her crayon.

   | do |

3. I have to _____ my story.

   | write |

4. Now I _____ my backpack every night.

   | check |

5. I am very _____ about it, too.

   | happy |

6. My things are _____ around my sister.

   | safe |

▶ **Print** one word that means the same as each pair of words.

7. not cooked _____

8. not safe _____

9. not able _____

10. not kind _____

11. spell again _____

12. use again _____

13. play again _____

14. tell again _____

Add the prefix **un** or **re** to each underlined word. **Print the new word on the line.**

1 to <u>read</u> again

_____

2 opposite of <u>lock</u>

_____

3 to <u>fill</u> again

_____

4 opposite of <u>tie</u>

_____

5 opposite of <u>buckle</u>

_____

6 to <u>heat</u> again

_____

7 to <u>build</u> again

_____

8 opposite of <u>pack</u>

_____

9 to <u>write</u> again

_____

10 opposite of <u>happy</u>

_____

11 to <u>play</u> again

_____

12 to <u>wind</u> again

_____

Home

Write prefixes (*re-*, *un-*) and base words on separate cards. Match them to make new words.

Name _____

> ▶ Add **dis** to the word beside each sentence. Use the new words to finish the sentences.

RULE

The prefix **dis** also means the opposite of the original word. Add **dis** to the base word **order** to make **disorder**.

1. My dog Wags _____ for a while. | appeared |

2. Then I _____ my shoe was missing. | covered |

3. "Why did you _____ me, Wags?" | obey |

4. "You know I'm _____ when you take my things." | pleased |

5. "That was a _____ thing to do." | loyal |

6. "Wags, you are a _____." | grace |

7. Wags barked to _____. | agree |

8. He pulled my shoe out of my

_____ toy chest. | orderly |

THINK! What did the boy think happened to his shoe?

Lesson 105
Prefix dis-

225

Fill in the bubble beside the word that will finish each sentence. Write the word on the line.

1	Mr. Fixit will _____ the plug before fixing the telephone.	○ discolor ○ disconnect
2	The rider will _____ and let her horse rest.	○ dismount ○ distaste
3	Meg and Peg are twin sisters, but they _____ about many things.	○ disagree ○ disappear
4	The puppy _____ its owner and ran outside with her hat.	○ dishonest ○ disobeyed
5	Will loves green beans, but he _____ eggplant.	○ dislikes ○ disgrace
6	Kirk made the dirt appear, so he had to make it _____ .	○ disappear ○ distrust

226 Lesson 105
Prefix dis-

Home Take turns making up sentences for the unused *dis-* words on this page.

Name _____

un or dis		re or dis	
1. _____ agree	2. _____ happy	7. _____ able	8. _____ writes
3. _____ obey	4. _____ easy	9. _____ new	10. _____ like
5. _____ lucky	6. _____ please	11. _____ pay	12. _____ loyal

▶ Add **un, dis,** or **re** to each underlined word to change the
meaning of the sentence. Print the new word on the line.

13. Grandpa was <u>pleased</u> about
the plans for his party.   _____

14. He said he felt <u>easy</u> about
getting gifts.   _____

15. Sadly Sue <u>wrapped</u> the
present she had made.   _____

16. Then Jake said they would
<u>obey</u> Grandpa just once.   _____

17. With a grin, Sue <u>wrapped</u>
the gift.   _____

18. She <u>tied</u> the bow.   _____

19. Grandpa was not <u>happy</u>
with his party after all.   _____

► **Draw a line** from the prefix to a base word to make a new word. **Write** the word on the line.

un	read
dis	happy
re	obey

1. _____

2. _____

3. _____

dis	easy
re	agree
un	pay

4. _____

5. _____

6. _____

► Add **un, dis,** or **re** to the base word to make a word that will finish the sentence. **Write** the new word on the line.

7.	Amber will _____ her gift.	wrap
8.	Alex and Max _____.	agree
9.	Rita will _____ the house.	build
10.	Taro is never _____ to animals.	kind
11.	Look! The ice is still _____.	safe
12.	My baby sister _____ rice.	likes
13.	The magician made the bird _____.	appear

 Home Use the new words in the boxes at the top of the page in sentences.

Name _____

See all the gifts and presents we wrapped?
It's easy and simple to do.
Little and small, big and large,
Here's a box for you!

RULE

Synonyms are words that have the same or almost the same meaning. **Gifts** and **presents** mean the same thing.

▶ **Print** each word from the box beside a word that means the same thing.

1. big _____	2. small _____
3. happy _____	4. quick _____
5. sick _____	6. wet _____

glad
ill
damp
fast
little
large

▶ **Circle** the word in each row that means the same as the first word.

7. **jolly**	sad	big	happy	jump
8. **junk**	gems	trash	list	top
9. **pile**	heap	near	rest	stop
10. **sleep**	awake	nap	paint	read
11. **sick**	ill	quick	lazy	glad
12. **quick**	step	slow	pony	fast
13. **sound**	sad	noise	find	happy
14. **large**	huge	many	tiny	blue
15. **close**	move	let	shut	see

Finish Peggy's letter. Print a word from the box that means the same thing as the word below each line.

friend	happy
gifts	races
noise	easy
fast	big
hope	little
kind	enjoy
laugh	

Dear Pablo,

I'm _____ that you came to my
_____glad_____

party. It was _____ of you to bring _____.
_____nice_____   _____presents_____

The _____ book looks _____ to read. I will
_____large_____   _____simple_____

_____ reading it. When I wind up the _____
_____like_____   _____small_____

robot, it _____ _____ and makes a funny
_____runs_____   _____quickly_____

_____. It makes me _____ to watch it.
_____sound_____   _____giggle_____

Thank you very much. I _____ to see you soon.
_____wish_____

Your _____,
_____pal_____

Peggy

Why did Peggy write to Pablo?

Home Ask your child to read Peggy's letter to you.

Name _____

Hot or cold, rain or shine,
My dog likes the backyard best.
Day or night, summer or winter,
He needs a place to rest.

▶ Find **a word in the box that means the opposite of each word.** Print **its letter on the line.**

a. **old**	b. **wet**	c. **start**	d. **full**	e. **slow**
f. **last**	g. **down**	h. **hot**	i. **good**	j. **short**
k. **out**	l. **well**	m. **few**	n. **winter**	o. **long**
p. **far**	q. **lower**	r. **shallow**	s. **shut**	t. **awake**
u. **thick**	v. **fat**	w. **white**	x. **hard**	

1. _____ dry   2. _____ up   3. _____ summer   4. _____ short

5. _____ near   6. _____ fast   7. _____ tall   8. _____ bad

9. _____ cold   10. _____ thin   11. _____ sick   12. _____ many

13. _____ stop   14. _____ upper   15. _____ first   16. _____ deep

17. _____ new   18. _____ empty   19. _____ open   20. _____ in

21. _____ asleep   22. _____ easy   23. _____ black   24. _____ skinny

Print a word from the box that means the opposite of each word and describes the picture.

stop	open	full	ill	cry	night
float	hot	strong	asleep	sit	smile

1 awake

2 close

3 empty

_____

_____

_____

4 cold

5 healthy

6 stand

_____

_____

_____

7 weak

8 sink

9 day

_____

_____

_____

10 laugh

11 frown

12 go

_____

_____

_____

Home Take turns using each antonym pair in a sentence.

Name _____

Grandma will sew a blue-green quilt
So everyone can see
How the wind blew the boats about
On a stormy day at sea.

Find a word in the box that sounds the same as each word below. Print the word on the line.

tail	here	to	road	pail	heal
blue	week	cent	sail	maid	sea

1. heel _____

2. see _____

3. rode _____

4. sent _____

5. tale _____

6. blew _____

7. weak _____

8. pale _____

9. hear _____

10. two _____

11. sale _____

12. made _____

Circle the word that will finish each sentence. Print it on the line.

13. Maggie _____ her horse into the woods.   road   rode

14. Her puppy wagged its _____ and ran along.   tail   tale

15. They saw a _____ that hid behind a tree.   dear   deer

16. Maggie watched the _____ set in the west.   son   sun

Find a word in the box that sounds the same as each word below. **Print** it on the line.

son	meat	blew
to	pane	tow
tale	week	heel
wait	beet	cent
sea	dear	sew

1. weight _____

2. sun _____

3. weak _____

4. sent _____

5. blue _____

6. beat _____

7. deer _____

8. two _____

9. heal _____

10. pain _____

11. see _____

12. meet _____

13. so _____

14. tail _____

15. toe _____

Use words from the box and the activity above to **finish** the sentences.

16. It had rained all _____.

17. When Pete woke up, the _____ was shining.

18. He could _____ his friends playing outside.

19. He pulled on his _____ jeans in a hurry.

20. He ran out _____ fly his kite.

Lesson 109
Homonyms

Home

Help your child write each homonym on a card or paper and then match them.

Name _____

Phonics & Spelling

▶ Read the words in the box. Then write two words that belong under each heading.

Words That Mean the Same Thing

_____   _____

Words That Sound the Same

_____   _____

Words That Are Opposites

_____   _____

Words That Begin with dis-

_____   _____

Words That Begin with un-

_____   _____

Words That Begin with re-

_____   _____

Word List

rewrite
dislike
hot
little
reread
undo
cold
deer
dear
disagree
unhappy
small

Prefixes, synonyms, antonyms, homonyms: Spelling

Phonics & Writing

Write about your favorite color. Why do you like it? What comes in this color? How does it make you feel? Use some of the words in the box.

unusual
little
hot
cold
glad
disagree
dislike
hard
easy
discover

Book Corner

Making a Plate
by Jennifer Jacobson

Potter Sam Salas shows how to make a plate beginning with a lump of wet clay and ending with a finished piece.

Home

Ask your child to read his or her writing to you.

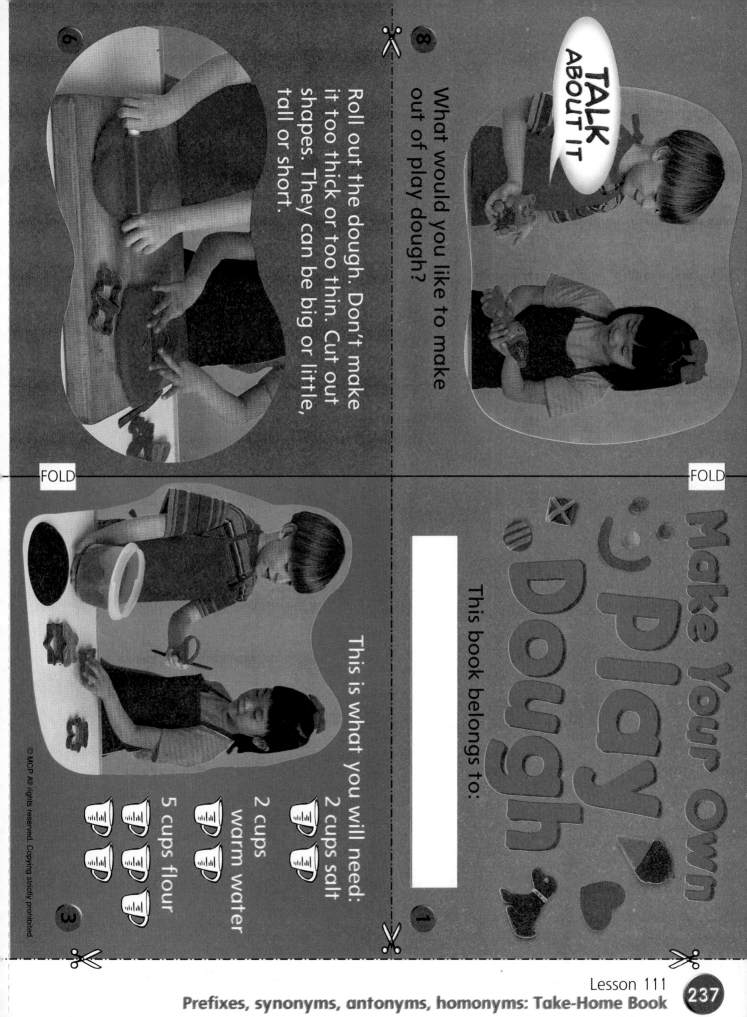

6

Roll out the dough. Don't make it too thick or too thin. Cut out shapes. They can be big or little, tall or short.

FOLD

8

What would you like to make out of play dough?

TALK ABOUT IT

FOLD

1

This book belongs to:

Make Your Own Play Dough

3

This is what you will need:

2 cups salt

2 cups warm water

5 cups flour

It is unlikely
you will have
any dough
left over. But
if you do, you
can reuse it
later.

Knead and
reknead
the dough
until it is
smooth
and even.

FOLD

FOLD

You can make your own play dough.
It is easy and simple to do!

Mix the salt, flour, and water.
Add a cup of water. Refill the cup
and add more water if you need it.

Lesson 111
Prefixes, synonyms, antonyms, homonyms: Take-Home Book

Name _____

Circle two words in each box that mean the same thing.

1	cold cool seed shook	2	hair small little home	3	fast fell quick queen
4	three tree shut close	5	jump leap drink drop	6	sick snow ill blow

Circle two words in each box that mean the opposite.

7	little puppy jelly big	8	fly old new penny	9	bad candy rich good
10	they fast play slow	11	from dirty clean funny	12	asleep play baby awake

Circle the word that will finish each sentence. Print it on the line.

13. The _____ was shining.   sun   son

14. I put on my _____ shorts and blue hat.   read   red

15. I went for a sail on the _____.   see   sea

16. The wind blew the _____.   sails   sales

17. It almost _____ my hat off, too.   blew   blue

18. I had a _____ time!   grate   great

Lesson 112

239

Prefixes, synonyms, antonyms, homonyms: Checkup

Fill in the bubble beside the word that names or describes each picture.

1
○ tale
○ tell
○ tail

2
○ heel
○ hail
○ heal

3
○ day
○ deer
○ dear

4
○ rode
○ rod
○ road

5
○ sun
○ son
○ soon

6
○ knows
○ nose
○ now

Read the words. Fill in the bubble next to the word that has the same meaning.

7 opposite of wrap
○ unwrap
○ rewrap

8 to play again
○ replay
○ display

9 opposite of mount
○ dismount
○ remount

10 opposite of appear
○ reappear
○ disappear

11 spell again
○ dispell
○ respell

12 to tie again
○ untie
○ retie

13 opposite of like
○ dislike
○ relike

14 opposite of do
○ redo
○ undo

15 to pack again
○ repack
○ unpack

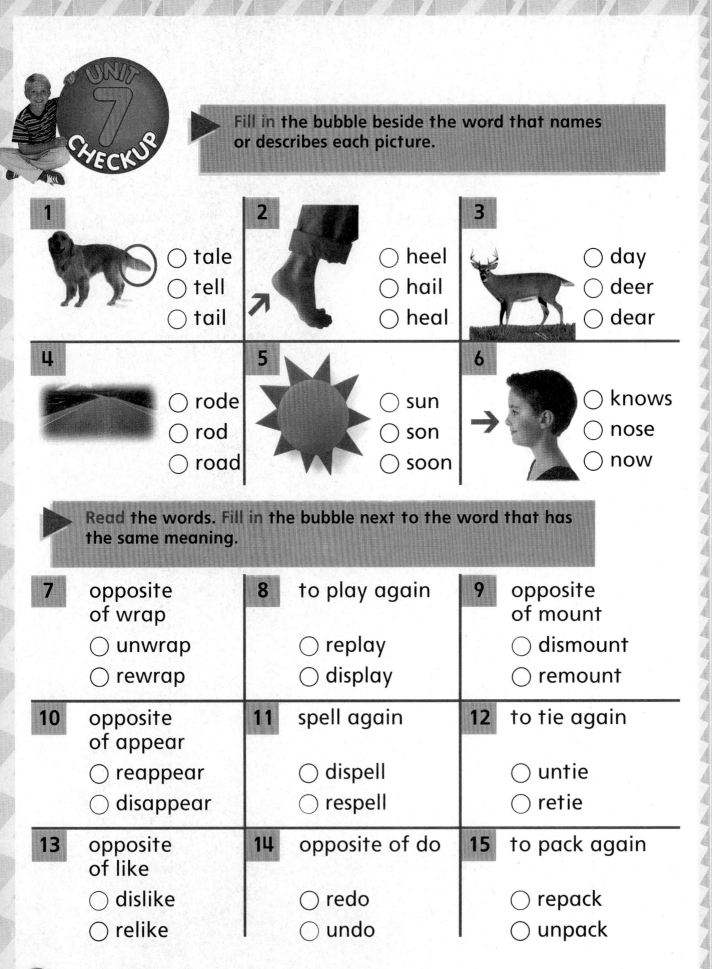